dark brown is the river

a memoir

Ruth Mugridge Snodgrass

Library of Congress Control Number: 2004095231

ISBN 0-9754867-0-5

Publisher's Cataloging-in-Publication
(Provided by Quality Books, Inc.)

Snodgrass, Ruth Mugridge.
   Dark brown is the river : a memoir / by Ruth Mugridge Snodgrass.
   p. cm.
   ISBN 0-9754867-0-5

   1. Snodgrass, Ruth Mugridge. 2. Somerset County (Pa.)—Biography. 3. Depressions—1929—Pennsylvania. 4. Nineteen thirties. 5. Floods—Pennsylvania—Johnstown. 6. Family—Pennsylvania—Somerset County. I. Title.

F157.S6S66 2004   974.8'79042'092
                      QB133-2050

♻ This book is printed on acid-free paper.

Printed in the U. S. A. by
Morris Publishing
3212 East Highway 30
Kearney, Nebraska 68847
800-650-7888

Dedicated to Gwen,
the little sister of my early years,
who grew up to be my best friend

~ Doris Gwendolyn Mugridge ~
1930-2003

Photographs

Front cover: The Stoneycreek in Hollsopple, Pennsylvania (2003)
Photo by Mary Buckley

Page iii: My sister Gwen with her beloved cat, Mosey (*circa* 1993)
Photo by Sharon Johnson

Pages x-xi: Photos of James Thomas Mugridge, Elizabeth Mugridge Greig, J. Robert Mugridge, and me courtesy of Marcy Zeppernick

Photo of Jeanne Mugridge McFarland courtesy of Denice Hanke

Back cover: Recent photo of me (2003) by Mary Buckley

Contents

Preface

When I started to write this memoir of my family, childhood friends, and events of the 1930's, such as the Johnstown Flood of 1936, I realized that I had to *imagine* conversations in order to enliven narratives, *interpret* motivation, and *search out* details that I hadn't thought about when I was simply *telling* my stories. And a funny thing happened as I immersed myself in memories, imagination, and research: I began to recall more and more.

I found myself understanding unexpected things about my parents: their feelings and their problems, their support of each other, their quietness and humor.

Having to check on flood facts that I was rather hazy about caused me to recollect related images and happenings that soon multiplied and flourished, as in Chapters 8 and 9.

Apparently, this expansion of memories is a common phenomenon for writers of this genre. Not long ago I was gratified to hear a quotation from Eudora Welty that describes my own experience: "As we discover, we remember; remembering, we discover." This collection of stories is the result of my remembering and discovering.

Acknowledgments

I'm happy to come from a family of storytellers, who have helped to preserve and reinforce memories of people, places, and events that continue to delight and strengthen me.

Thanks to nieces, Denice (Shonsa) Hanke and Marcy Zeppernick, who hunted through boxes and albums to provide old photos that I hadn't seen for years; to my son-in-law, Matt Buckley, for probing questions and satisfying discussions; and to great-nephew, Bryan Zeppernick, whose thoughtful reading suggested a more effective order of chapters. In fact, the enthusiastic reception of my stories by all of my family has proven to be a great energizer.

I'm also grateful to my niece, Denise Spencer, who drove us to Hollsopple, Pennsylvania, for the purpose of renewing old acquaintances and reviewing events of the 1930's. I appreciate the contributions of friends who still live in Hollsopple, who reminded me of the hard times and the good times we all lived through during the Great Depression. I enjoyed especially my conversations with Betty Helsel Blough, Sophia Zbrozek Katarski, and Beattie Shaffer Vatavuk and the memories they shared of my parents, brothers, sisters, and the town.

One of the greatest benefits I've experienced since starting to write this book has been a stronger contact with my brother Bob, my only remaining sibling. We've had long conversations, face to face and on the telephone, more, I think, than in all our adult lives up to now. He has traveled back with me to our small hometown and to our childhood; I cherish both journeys and can't thank him enough for them.

I'm indebted to friends at the Strasburg United Methodist Church who listened to or read my stories and encouraged me to continue writing them, especially Bill Bullock, whose comments and criticism were fresh, insightful, and valuable. A long-time teacher, Kathryn Gardner Weber, came to my aid when I needed details about school in the 1930's, especially the use of the hectograph. I'm really thankful to her for that, since she brought back into focus many otherwise fuzzy classroom memories.

I was very fortunate in meeting Joe McLaughlin, teacher, mentor, published author and poet, who generously shares his understanding of the creative process and publishing. His advice was instrumental in helping me to get my book published. I'm very grateful to him.

Joe's passion for writing and mentoring has resulted in the creation of the Tuscarawas County Writers' Guild, which I have found both educational and delightful. I've really enjoyed the contact with other aspiring writers, in particular, the members of the memoir group, who share with me the pleasure of telling our family tales, and of listening and laughing together.

I owe so much to my niece, Nancy Mugridge, who combined her computer expertise with her love of family lore to assist me in preparing the manuscript for publication. She was tireless in her work with photographs, fonts, and formatting, fighting time-zone differences and fatigue. I treasure the closeness that has continued to grow during the work on this book.

My daughter Mary has heard these stories all her life, so there's no one better qualified to ensure their survival in our family history. She brought a lively respect for language and expression to the job of editing. I appreciate her loving concern for the book and the opportunity to spend a lot of time working together, visiting Hollsopple and Johnstown, introducing her to the present-day towns she had already met through my stories. Thank you, Mary.

Ruth Snodgrass

These family stories are the product of both my memory and my imagination. I hope you will forgive any discrepancies in time, place, names, or events and consider them unintentional or relatively unimportant. For instance, my brother Bob and I have had to agree to disagree on several items.

An Introduction to the Mugridges

My Parents:

James Thomas Mugridge
(1891 – 1944)

married 1913

Mary Reese Mugridge
(1889 – 1976)

Their Children:

Elizabeth ("Sister") (1914 – 1995)

1935 married James I. Greig (1916 – 1979)

3 Children: James (b. 1937), Robert (b. 1939), and Marcy (b. 1942)

John (1918 – 1985)

1943 married Esther Long (b. 1921)

2 Children: Cheryl (b. 1946) and James (b. 1949)

J. Robert (b. 1922)

1948 married Olga E. Moore (1926 – 2001)

6 Children: Sharon (b. 1948), Nancy (b. 1950), Paul (b. 1954), David (b. 1959), Denise (b. 1959), and Rebecca (b. 1963)

Jeanne (1925 – 1966)

1948 married Robert W. McFarland (1918 –1996)

1 Child: Denice (b. 1952)

Ruth (b. 1928)

1969 married John Snodgrass (b. 1929) (div.)

1 Child: Mary (b. 1971)

Gwendolyn ("Denny") (1930–2003)

dark brown is the river

1

FARAWAY ACROSS THE YARD

We were eating breakfast one very cold winter morning when a small knock sounded at the back door. Mother was dishing up hot cereal into our bowls and asked me to go to the door. I opened it and found Thelma Shaffer, a girl about my age, seven or eight, standing on the steps. She must have run across the yard without a coat or jacket, for she stood there on the steps shivering and pulling a skimpy sweater around her as tightly as she could. Thelma hadn't been in school the past few days, so I was especially happy to see her.

"Hi," I said, and took a bite of the buttered toast I had carried with me.

"Hi," she said, eyeing the toast.

"Who is it, Ruth?" Mother called.

"It's Thelma Shaffer," I answered, wanting to take another bite but didn't.

"Well, Ruth, tell her to come in. It's too cold to stand out there."

"Mother says to come in," I told Thelma.

"My ma said not to. I have to talk to your ma," Thelma said, wiping her nose on her sleeve.

Mother came to the door. "What's the matter, Thelma?" she asked. "Is something wrong with the baby?" Mrs. Shaffer often came over to get help with a sick child, maybe one-year-old Catherine, or Cacky, as her five older brothers and sisters called her. This had happened more often in the months since Mr. Shaffer died in the explosion at the small, one-man coal mine he operated.

Things were hard for everyone in the Depression, but they were really bad for a young woman left with six children. Our mother tried to help her as much as she could with food and hand-me-down clothes, medicine, and advice, so this morning's visit was not unusual.

"What's the matter, Thelma?" Mother repeated. "Come on in. It's too cold to stand out there."

Thelma shook her head. "Ma said not to come in. She said to ask you if you'd come over and start the fire. She's sick in bed and there's nothing to eat." She looked again at my toast but didn't say anything.

Mother thought for a minute. "Thelma, tell your mother I'll be right over. I just have to get the children off to school. Here, wait a minute," she said as Thelma turned to go. "Here's something to eat until I get there," and she wrapped a loaf of homemade bread in a tea towel and handed it to the shivering girl. "I'll be there in a few minutes." Thelma took the bread and, hugging it to her, ran down the steps and across the frozen grass to the old frame house.

Mother turned to the rest of us seated at the long kitchen table. "Bobby, take a basket of wood over to their house and just leave it on the porch. I'll take it in when I go over. Jeanne, stop at the store and tell your dad to get some food together right away and have someone take it to the house."

"What kind of stuff?" Jeanne asked.

"Oh, he'll know," Mother replied. "A soup bone and vegetables. Mother's Oats. Milk. Bread."

"You gave them bread," reminded Gwen.

"That'll be gone before I get over there," said Mother. "I'll bet they're really hungry."

She glanced at the big kettle of cookies that usually sat on the counter. "I'll just take these with me. Those kids don't get cookies very often." She pulled on her heavy sweater and then her coat. "Your lunches are ready. Jeanne, see that everybody has everything. Tell your daddy that I want those things right away for the Shaffers. He can just leave them on the porch." A brief hug and she was out the door. Parents weren't so demonstrative in their dealings with their children in those days. No "I love you" at every minor parting.

We got ready and went to school. We found out later what happened at the Shaffers'.

When Mother went in the door, there was no one downstairs. Even Thelma had crawled back in bed with her brothers and sisters, along with Baby Cacky. They had torn off pieces of the bread that Mother had sent over and were trying to eat and keep warm at the same time. When Mother called from the foot of the stairs that she was there, they got up and straggled down to the kitchen in their cold, bare feet to watch her build a fire in the black kitchen stove.

While the fire was beginning to take hold, she enlisted the help of the older girls in getting the two little boys and the baby dressed in the threadbare bits of clothing she found. She had been right about the loaf of bread; it was gone by the time the oatmeal was ready to eat. After the hot cereal and cups of half-milk, half-tea, the children were happy to be settled, warm and cozy under a faded quilt on the sofa.

Then Mother decided to go up and see Mrs. Shaffer. She got a towel and wet washcloth, fixed a small dish of oatmeal and a cup of tea, and went upstairs. She turned on the light, a single bulb hanging in the center of the dark room. "Good morning, Mrs. Shaffer," said Mother. "I hear you're not feeling very well." She set the tray on a chair beside the bed.

"Good morning, Mrs. Mugridge." Mrs. Shaffer's voice was barely a whisper, her face a pale shadow. "I'm real sick."

"I can see that," said Mother. "Well, let me wash your hands and face and plump up your pillows. I know that always makes me feel better when I'm under the weather." Mrs. Shaffer didn't resist Mother's ministrations but lay passive and miserable while Mother bent over her. She managed just a few spoonfuls of thin oatmeal and a couple sips of tea before she turned her face away.

"Mrs. Shaffer...Edna," Mother tried to speak cheerfully, "you have to eat a little more. You need to get strong to take care of your children." No response. "Mrs. Shaffer, has the doctor been here?" A whispered yes. "When was he here?"

"About an hour ago."

"Did he tell you what's wrong with you?"

"Yes," came the reply. "I have diphtheria."

Mother was stunned. "The doctor says you have diphtheria?"

"Yes."

"When did you say he was here?" Mother asked, still not quite believing.

"A little while ago," Mrs. Shaffer murmured weakly. "I sent Thelma for him."

Mother imagined the thin, hungry eight-year-old racing to the doctor's house about a block away at seven in the morning, probably in that same inadequate sweater she had worn to our house. "Edna," she persisted, "diphtheria is really contagious. I don't think I can go home to my family. Did Dr. Zimmerman tell you to get me?"

"No," Mrs. Shaffer whispered, "he just said to try to get someone to start the fire. Thelma could take care of me, but there wasn't any wood to start a fire. That's all I wanted you to do. I didn't think you would come upstairs. I'm real sorry, Mrs. Mugridge," and she started to cry.

"Don't cry, Edna," Mother said, although she felt like crying herself. "Is the doctor coming back this morning?"

"Yes, he said he was going to give the kids some kind of shot so that if they got the diphtheria, it wouldn't be so bad. Mrs. Mugridge," there was the slightest note of hope in the sick woman's voice, "maybe he could give you a shot, too, and you could go home."

"Maybe you're right," said Mother, trying to keep her hopes up. "Because I have a family to take care of, too." Neither one mentioned that Mother also had the help of a husband and several teenage children, plus her own eighty-six-year-old mother, who was still very good at holding children, singing to them and telling them stories. "Try to rest before the doctor comes. I'll go down and get some soup started. Your kids will like that, I know." She patted Mrs. Shaffer's hand. "Maybe it's not as bad as we think."

The doctor returned later that morning and gave something he called "toxin-antitoxin" to the children and to our mother in the form of shots. However, Mother was not permitted to come home. Dr. Zimmerman stopped in at the store and told our dad not to expect to see his wife for some time.

"Can she come home at night when the kids are in bed?" Daddy asked. "You know, to get clothes, or to wash her clothes, or let me know what she wants me to do about household problems or the children?"

The short answer was no. "But you can talk across the yard when you need to. You can put clean clothes on the porch for her."

Daddy thought about this. "Can we wash her clothes? We don't have an endless supply of clean clothes."

"I'm not sure about that," said the doctor. "I'll find out."

When we got home from school that day to a motherless house, our father was there to explain the situation. Gwen and I were indignant. "Thelma came over here and took our mother," complained Gwen. "That's not right."

"Why didn't she get someone who doesn't have kids?" I argued. "Someone that no one needs."

"You two say such dumb things sometimes," said Jeanne. "Mrs. Shaffer is really sick. Thelma didn't just *decide* to steal our mother."

"That's right," said Daddy. "She just wanted to have someone to make a fire. That house must have been freezing. Can't you imagine how cold it must have been?"

"Why didn't she get a fireman then?" Gwen whined. The rest of us laughed, and Gwen was so delighted to think she had made a joke that she said it again. "Why didn't she get a fireman?"

Jeanne had an idea. "Daddy, what are they having for supper?"

"Soup. She was going to make a big kettle of soup," he answered. "That'll probably be enough for a couple of meals."

"Well, we can't do it tonight, but tomorrow, why don't we have the same meal that Mother fixes for them?"

"Just tell me what you want to make, and I'll send the same stuff to their house," Daddy agreed. "What do you want for tomorrow?"

"How about macaroni and cheese?" she suggested.

"Okay," he said. "Everybody likes that. Can you make it?"

"Grandma can probably help me," Jeanne replied.

I thought of something else. "Where will she sleep? They have just three beds."

"She'll probably sleep on the sofa," said Jeanne, "but she'll need blankets."

"I can take some over and leave them on the porch," said our brother Bobby. "Do we have some we don't need?"

"Daddy," asked Jeanne, "can blankets be contagious?"

"I'm not sure about diphtheria," he replied, "but for some contagious diseases, the health department requires that bedclothes be burned."

"Can't she just wash them when she gets home?" I wondered.

Bobby came back from the laundry room where he had been for a few minutes. "Hey, come out to the door. Mother's looking out the Shaffers' window! Maybe she's looking for us."

We ran to the door and crowded together at the window. "Wave! Wave!" said Jeanne. "I think she sees us." We waved vigorously, and across the way the woman in the window waved back.

"She's holding the baby," announced Gwen. "That's Baby Cacky."

"I'll bet the baby misses her mother," said Jeanne. "Mrs. Shaffer is probably not allowed to hold her."

Or feed her, I thought. I could not have imagined bringing up the

subject or saying the word "breast-feeding," but I wondered just
the same.

Gwen moved away from the window. "I'm going to see what
Grandma's doing," she said. She was only five, going-on six, the
baby of our family. Maybe she missed her mother, too.

Every day, many times a day, one or more of us could be found at
the window of the back door, searching, hoping for a sign of our
mother. Gwen and I would also stand on the commode in the upstairs
bathroom and look out the small window, especially at night. "I'll
bet Mother hates it over there," Gwen said once.

"Why?" asked Grandma, who was helping us get ready for bed.

"'Cause they don't have a bathroom inside," she answered. "She
has to go down to the outhouse in the daytime, and at night she has
to use that pitcher thing—what do you call it, Grandma?"

"A slop jar," Grandma replied, and Gwen and I both made faces.
"Well, that's what we had when your mother was growing up, so it's
nothing new to her."

"Well, anyway, she doesn't have to empty it," I said. "That's
Thelma's job."

"That little girl has a hard life," Grandma commented, "taking
care of her sisters and brothers so much of the time, helping do
housework, plus trying to do her own schoolwork. She deserves a
medal."

"She doesn't get good grades, Grandma," I said. "Miss Miller
says she doesn't study."

"No wonder," Grandma defended her. "When would she have
time?"

I didn't say anything. This was a new thought for me.

"When all this is over, Ruth," Grandma went on, "you could probably help her with what she is missing. You can play school."
Grandma knew how to appeal to me; she knew I had already decided
to be a teacher. "Beattie, too. They'll need lots of help. It might be
fun for you."

"Yeah, maybe." I didn't want to admit it, but it did sound interesting. I opened the small window and leaned out as far as I could
for our nightly ritual.

"Move over. Give me room," said Gwen, leaning out beside me.

"Good night, Mother!" we hollered. "Good night, Shaffers!" The
bright rectangle of a window in the small house suddenly filled with

silhouetted heads and arms of children waving. A larger figure appeared holding a baby.

"There's our mother," whispered Gwen. The window was pushed up and the kids across the way leaned out and yelled back, "Good night, Mugridges!"

The laundry problem was resolved by having the Shaffers' clothing washed at our house, but separately from ours to avoid any possible contagion. Also, it was a considerable chore to pump and heat all the water needed, and Dad wanted to spare Mother whatever he could. When Gwen and I placed the Shaffers' wet socks on the radiator as we usually did with our own, I counted them and realized that they wore one pair for at least three days each. When Elizabeth, our oldest sister, showed Daddy the poor collection of underwear, socks, moth-eaten sweaters, skirts, pants, and sad little shirts that Mother had gathered, he contacted the Red Cross and told them the situation. In a day or so, several boxes of clothing were delivered to the Shaffers' porch, in addition to good used sheets and blankets. And then stuff began to arrive from neighbors: kettles of soup, meatloaves, cookies, homemade bread, apples, and warm children's clothes, all left on the porch, anonymously, except for the kettles.

"It's like Christmas, Grandma," I marveled, and she agreed.

Finally, after twenty-one days, the quarantine was lifted and our mother came home. We had not been notified beforehand, so when Jeanne and I got home from school, we were amazed to find Mother sitting on the sofa, holding Gwen on her lap and and reading her a story. Oh, how we hugged and kissed her as though she had been on a long journey to a faraway place and not just across the yard in a neighbor's house. We sat there for a little while and then Jeanne asked, "Is Mrs. Shaffer better now, Mother?"

"She's not contagious now, but she's still really weak and tired. I made enough mush for supper that there'll still be a lot left for tomorrow. Her sister is going to stay for about a month. Edna won't have too much to do, just rest." Mother got up and walked to the kitchen, saying, "Well, what'll *we* have for supper tonight?" She laughed when we each shouted our favorites. We followed her out to the laundry to get the sack of potatoes, and I saw her look out the window in the direction of the Shaffers' house. Her glance lingered for just a moment before she went back to the kitchen.

"Mother," Jeanne asked, "what did you do all day over there?"

"Oh," she answered, "I kept busy. I got the meals and took care of Mrs. Shaffer. I made sure the fire didn't go out. Oh, and I took care of the baby."

"Did you do the dishes?" I asked. This was the job I disliked.

"No," she replied, "Thelma and Beattie did them every meal. They were a big help."

Mother never got diphtheria herself, and that was all she told us right then about her stay with the Shaffers. Over time, however, we learned a little more. Thelma came back to school and knew her spelling words and arithmetic problems as though she had never missed a day. Once at recess I saw her try to show another girl Fly Away, Jack! Fly Away, Jim!, a game involving little pieces of paper stuck with spit to the fingertips. I didn't think anyone else knew that but us. And then in the summer, on rainy days when the neighborhood kids played on our porch, I often saw the younger Shaffer kids, especially Danny and Emory, sitting close to Mother on the swing, or dozing, one on each side of her with their heads on her lap and her arms gently curving around them, her feet now and then touching the porch floor and giving the swing a little push.

Mother (circa *1913*) *This unusual photograph may have been taken at a going-away party before her wedding.*

2

SUMMER OF THE DANCE

"Mother," I whispered, "Jeanne just stabbed me in the arm with her fork!"

Our sister Jeanne was almost finished with third grade when I started noticing her shaking and jerking. I was four, going-on five, so I was puzzled by her odd behavior: suddenly splashing her milk on me at the table, stabbing herself with a forkful of vegetables, or lurching and falling on a perfectly level sidewalk. A glance at our mother stopped my questions for the moment. *Don't say anything* was the message I clearly understood. When I had Mother to myself, I pressed her for the reason for Jeanne's odd behavior. "The doctor thinks she has a really strange sickness," Mother tried to explain, "but he's not sure."

"What is it?" I asked.

"St. Vitus' Dance," she replied. "It's a disease children get that causes them to lose control of their muscles and shake really badly."

"She's getting worse," I said. "Will she get better? Will she always be like this?" I felt a terrible hurting sadness for my sister.

"Dr. Grazier says that since school will be out next week, she can finish the year and then he'll start giving her a really strong medicine." Mother paused for a second before going on. "Then we'll be able to tell."

"Can she still be in the circus?" I asked. On the last afternoon of school the children were going to put on their version of a circus, taking the parts of animals and trainers, acrobats, clowns, and dancers in wonderful costumes that the mothers had made of crepe paper and scraps of material. Jeanne was to wear a costume that I thought was especially marvelous: it started with an old bathing suit that had bright, fringy paper flowers stitched to the top and a little gathered skirt of red crepe paper with a scalloped edge. A short yellow cape of crepe paper completed the outfit. I secretly hoped that I would inherit the costume when Jeanne outgrew it.

In addition, our little Boston bulldog, Lady,[1] was to be a lion with a tangled gold crepe paper mane. She was extremely good-natured and could be counted on to roll over, play dead, and step, not jump, through a little hoop. Would the circus now be out of the picture for Jeanne?

"We'll see," said Mother. "We'll see how she feels next week."

Each passing day of that week brought increasing difficulties for our sister: more spills, falls, and tears. Mother tried to convince Jeanne that she didn't have to go to school the last few days, but she was determined to finish the year and take part in the circus. She turned in her books on the next-to-last day so she could stay home the next morning and arrive just in time for the circus parade.

So, after lunch, Elizabeth, whom we called Sister until the day she died at the age of 81, took off work at our father's store and drove us to the school. The car was packed full with Sister, Mother, Grandma, Jeanne, Gwen, and me, in addition to Lady, who sat on my lap in the back seat, already wearing her curly mane and taking a calm interest in people on the sidewalks, many moving in the direction of Hollsopple's[2] little three-room school on the hill. Our brother Bob was already at school, getting ready for the circus.

Sister was able to pull up close to where the children were lining up for the circus parade. Miss Miller, Jeanne's teacher, helped her out of the car and walked with her to her place in the line; I put the leash on Lady and took her over to Jeanne. After a brief struggle transferring the loop on the end of the leash from my hand to Jeanne's, I went back to the rest of the family sitting on the grassy edge of the playground.

Several high school students had been recruited to play a couple of horns and a drum; the music started, and the parade began. Three dogs dressed as jungle animals began to howl. Their owners pulled at their leashes and tried unsuccessfully to quiet them; the dogs seemed unable to walk and howl at the same time, so the parade line had to snake around them. Finally, the dogs simply stopped howling, joined the parade line, and walked meekly along beside their masters.

Miss Miller had told Jeanne that she didn't have to be in the parade if she wanted to rest until her act, but Jeanne thought she'd like to try walking with the other kids and animals. However, after about ten steps she stopped and looked at Miss Miller. I held my breath. Was she going to quit the circus? No, she just took Miss Miller's hand and sat down on a little chair to wait until the parade line came back around to the starting point again. I relaxed. It wouldn't be long now. Her teacher had arranged for Jeanne's act to be the first one.

The circus performers were finally back where they had started and were seated on benches, the animals on leashes at their masters' feet or in their arms. The music stopped, and the ringmaster, a tall eighth grade boy, stepped out to the center and swept a high black hat from his head. He was wearing a bright red shirt (a blouse of his mother's?) and black pants tucked into knee-high black rubber boots (borrowed from a fireman?). I was thrilled to hear him speak loudly with unfamiliar authority through a small megaphone, which he had borrowed from his older brother, a cheerleader.

"Ladies and gentlemen! Boys and girls! Teachers, cats, and dogs!" Everybody laughed. He went on: "It is my pleasure to welcome you to the BENSON BOROUGH BIG TOP!" The way he emphasized the last words made everyone clap enthusiastically. He raised his baton and continued: "Our first act features our talented animal trainer, Miss Jeanne Mugridge, and her wonderful Lady the Lion, who will perform for us feats of intelligence and agility. Here they are, MISS JEANNE AND LADY THE LION!" He turned to where Jeanne and Lady were waiting. I had been so charmed by the ringmaster that I hadn't looked at Jeanne for a few minutes. She must have been picking and pulling nervously at her skirt, for there at her feet were shreds and tears of crepe paper. She stood still, unable to move.

"Oh, dear," murmured Mother. Miss Miller seemed to be speaking quietly to Jeanne, encouraging her to walk to the middle of the playground.

I turned to Mother. "I can help her, Mother! I helped her practice with Lady. Let me go help her!"

Mother, unable to speak, nodded her permission, so I got up and walked quickly across the grass to my sister. I picked up the hoop with one hand and with the other captured Jeanne's jerking wrist. "Let's go, Jeanne," I whispered. "Bring Lady," and the three of us made our way to the center, haltingly. The audience of mothers, grandmothers, and young children was silent. The school children looked sideways at each other, not knowing what to think.

I unfastened the leash and patted our little dog on the head. "Start the first trick, Jeanne," I whispered. "Say 'sit.'" And she did. Jeanne gave commands in a shaky voice, but Lady knew what to do. She sat, begged, shook hands, rolled over, played dead with her legs sticking straight up in the air. I looked around at the crowd. With every trick the children laughed and clapped their hands. I was so proud of both of them!

I looked back at Jeanne and was horrified to see that she had started to jerk badly. With only one trick to go! Jeanne was looking at me in desperation. "I have to sit down. Please help me," she whispered. I grabbed her hand. "Bow!" I said, and somehow we managed to make it to the sidelines, followed by Lady acting very nervous and puzzled. Everybody hollered and cheered. We were able to make it to the benches before Jeanne collapsed.

Her mouth was trembling as she tried to speak, "Tell Mother I want to go home." I ran over to my family and told them what Jeanne had said. Sister got up immediately. "Ask Mr. Hadden to carry her to the car," she said as she helped Mother and Grandma to their feet.

I ran again to the benches and gave the message to the principal, who picked Jeanne up easily and carried her to our waiting car. Mother opened the door and he set Jeanne in on her lap. He tried to smooth the shreds of her little paper skirt. "I hope you feel better soon, Jeannie," he said. "You're a good lion tamer." She smiled faintly but didn't say anything. Mother wrapped her arms around her and caught her wildly jerking hands.

Lady and I clambered into the back seat with Gwen and Grandma. As the car started, I looked back at the playground, where the circus was going on without us. Two kids dressed as hobo clowns were chasing a little dog that had snatched one of their wigs; the crowd was laughing uproariously. I watched as long as I could before the car turned to go down the hill. We can teach Lady more tricks for next year, I thought, and settled back and smiled to myself.

When we got home, Sister helped Mother put Jeanne to bed while Grandma sat on the front porch swing with Gwen and me. Lady snoozed on a little rug nearby, no longer adorned with her golden mane. "It was nice of you to help Jeanne today," said Grandma. I nodded in agreement. "Was it fun to be in the circus?"

"Oh, yeah," I said. "When I'm in school, I'm going to be in the circus, too."

"Wasn't Lady good?" Grandma went on. Lady's ears flicked when she heard her name, and her little stub of a tail twitched, but she didn't get up; she just let out a big sigh. The three of us laughed, and then we sat there swinging, not saying anything.

Mother had told us the doctor was coming, but she hadn't said which one. We were still sitting on the swing when when Dr. Grazier showed up. Though it may seem odd today for such a small town to have supported two doctors, Holsopple and the communities, coal mines, and farms around it more than kept both physicians busy, especially with house calls and emergencies. As Dr. Grazier came up the porch steps, he greeted us but didn't stop to chat. "I know where to go," he said and headed upstairs to the bedroom Jeanne shared with Sister.

We continued sitting there, not saying much, just wondering now and then what the doctor was doing and whether Jeanne was going to be okay. Bobby had joined us on the porch by this time, not knowing what to do with himself. A sixth-grader, he had helped with props and scenery at the circus. He jumped when Dr. Grazier spoke his name and came out on the porch with a small square of paper. "Bobby, run down to the drugstore and get this prescription filled." Bobby was so relieved to be active that he was down the steps and out on the sidewalk before Mother called him back for the money, and then he was off again.

The medicine that Jeanne had to take really fascinated me. I watched Mother give it to her every day: one drop the first day, two drops the second, all the way up to ten drops the tenth day; then back down again, nine drops, eight drops, seven, until it was down to one drop on the nineteenth day. I'm not sure, but I think it started back up again, then down. It seemed to me that she slept most of the time, her hands flailing in her sleep. Mother got her up to go to the bathroom several times a day, partly for the exercise, but I don't think it helped much, since she had to have one person on each side, half carrying her.

When Jeanne was awake, there was always someone with her, reading, talking, singing, rubbing her back, or cooling her with damp washcloths in the humid summer air. What I did when I was with her was play with my paper dolls. I laid out each doll and its clothes on one side of Jeanne's bed and asked her opinion.

"Bunny Sue is having a party and I have to decide what everyone is wearing. Do you think she should wear her red or blue party dress?"

"Red!" yelled Gwen, who had come into the bedroom to watch. She always picked red, no matter what.

"It's Jeanne's choice, Denny," I said. This was our family name for Gwen. I was twenty months old when she was born, and my attempts to pronounce her name resulted in "Den," and it stuck.

"Pick red, Jeanne," she said.

"Okay, red," Jeanne sighed.

"Now," I went on, "which dress would Mary Lou wear, yellow or green?"

"I guess..." she started, but Gwen interrupted again with "Yellow!"

"All right, yellow," said Jeanne, turning away from us. "I'm tired now. I want to go to sleep."

I gathered up my paper dolls and their clothes and took them downstairs. "Mother," I asked, "where's Grandma? Jeanne doesn't want to play paper dolls."

"Well," said Mother, "I want you to do something else for me. Jeanne is so warm, I want to give her a bath to cool her off a little." She paused and I wondered what she wanted me to do. "Would you run up to Gloria Demmer's and ask whether she'd help me give Jeanne a bath? Tell her to wear her bathing suit, and come right away if she can." Gloria was Jeanne's best friend; she had come every day since school was out to inquire about Jeanne's health. I left the house immediately. I was sure Gloria would want to do something to help Jeanne.

I was right. Gloria's mother told her to put her bathing suit on and to go with me, and in just a few minutes the two of us were running over the railroad tracks and down to our end of town. I don't know exactly why we ran, except that we wanted so badly to do something for Jeanne, and there wasn't much we could do.

When Jeanne saw Gloria in her bathing suit, she decided she wanted to wear hers, too. So Grandma helped Mother dress Jeanne in the old swim suit that had been her circus outfit, paper flowers removed, of course. Gloria got into the empty tub first and sat down. Then Mother lifted Jeanne in and helped her sit down with her back to Gloria, who put her arms around her. Mother turned on the water, lukewarm, and added bubble bath; the water rose and the bubbles frothed around them. Jeanne's arms jerked and splashed, and the two girls shrieked with laughter. Mother's face was wet as she shampooed Jeanne's hair and rinsed it, filling a little pan with water from the spigot.

"Just relax, honey," she said, and finally Jeanne was able to lean back against Gloria, and Mother washed her all over. Then Gloria supported Jeanne while she half floated and played in the bubbly water. Finally, the water was let out, and the two girls were dried and helped out of the tub. Gloria decided to just wear her bathing suit home, but Jeanne was dressed in clean pajamas and put back to bed.

"Thank you, Gloria, for helping with Jeanne," said our mother. "Will you come again?"

"Oh, sure, that was fun," Gloria replied. "I'll come any day." She looked at Jeanne lying back against the pillow, her light brown hair curling around her face in damp ringlets. "Bye." My sister smiled her goodbye and nodded.

The baths became a fairly regular part of our lives, two or three times a week, and were the only happy times Jeanne had that summer. She didn't want to get out of bed or get dressed or play any board games that she once had enjoyed. The Fourth of July with its picnic and firecrackers aroused no interest in her; neither did my birthday at the end of the month. Mother expressed concern that, although the shaking and jerking had subsided, nothing appealed to Jeanne. "She needs to get active and stronger so she'll be ready for the beginning of school," I heard her say to Daddy.

It's funny how a one-cent coin marked Jeanne's return to health.

One morning I was lying on the floor in Jeanne's bedroom, coloring in a coloring book. I showed her my pictures now and then, but she wasn't much interested. All of a sudden Bobby ran into the room. "Look what I did!" he yelled. He held out a penny and came close to the bed so that Jeanne could see. There was a hole clear through the coin! I was so amazed I got up on my knees and tried to take it from him, but he held it closer to Jeanne.

"Look what I did!" he repeated.

"There's a hole in that penny!" she gasped. "How did you do that?"

"You won't believe it!" he answered. "I did it with a needle and a cork and a hammer!"

"Let me have it, Bobby! Please!" Jeanne begged. He held it out to her and dropped it into her outstretched hand. Her fingers closed over it. She slid to the edge of the bed and swung her legs to the floor. "Mother!" she called. "Mother!" She staggered to the door and started down the hall to Mother's room. "Look what Bobby did!"

We followed her to the doorway, surprised by the strength of her feelings, while Mother came out into the hall just in time to catch her. "Jeanne! What's the matter?"

Jeanne opened her hand. "Look what Bobby did!" she exclaimed. "He made a hole in this penny! I'm going down to show Grandma," and she started down the stairs for the first time in almost two months, holding on to the railing, it's true, then sitting and sliding on her bottom, but still, going somewhere under her own power and with enthusiasm. Mother held her breath until Jeanne got to the bottom, then turned to Bobby and me. Her eyes were really shiny. "I think she's going to get better now," she said, but her smile made her look as though she were about to cry.

Jeanne spent the rest of the day showing the penny to anyone who would take the time to look at it. She sat on the porch and called to neighbor kids, who were just as amazed as we were that you could make a hole in a penny with a needle and a cork. She could hardly wait until Sister, Dad, and John came home from the store for supper. Sister and Daddy were properly impressed, but John said, "You know it's illegal to deface coins of the United States of America, don't you? You can be put in jail for that."

Jeanne gasped and looked at Bobby. "Can you?"

"You can read what my *Boy's Life* magazine says," Bobby replied defiantly. "It doesn't say that."

Well, that penny brought Jeanne back into the flow of family life, and she became stronger day by day, so that when she asked Mother in a week or so if she could have a party to celebrate getting better, Mother was happy to agree.

Children's parties during the Depression were really low-key affairs. Jeanne's was no exception. About twelve to fifteen children from the neighborhood, plus Gloria Demmer and several of Jeanne's classmates from other parts of town, showed up promptly at two in the afternoon, and the games began. First, we played Lemonade, in which two teams took turns pantomiming various activities for the other team to guess. The guessers then chased the actors back to their home base, and claimed those they tagged. After fifteen minutes or so of this we moved on to Drop the Handkerchief and Prisoners' Base.

Then Mother, noticing some kids lying on the grass recovering from the vigorous running, brought out the refreshments. Everyone sat down on the lawn and ate cookies and drank lemonade very seriously. It was such a good party.

I looked around to see whether Jeanne was having a good time, but I couldn't find her. I was just about to go into the house when I saw her coming out the door with Lady. She was still wearing her shorts and top but had added the little cape of yellow crepe paper, and, somehow, Lady had a new curly mane. They stopped at an empty place on the grass, and Bobby came up and announced, "Miss Jeanne and Lady the Lion!" The kids were so surprised, there wasn't a sound.

Jeanne's voice was soft but not shaky as she gave the first command: "Lady, sit." Lady sat down and looked up at her as though she could hardly wait for the next command, wiggling a little.

And so they went through the tricks, with Jeanne's voice getting stronger as she went: beg, shake hands, roll over, play dead, and then the last command for the trick she had been unable to announce months before, "Lady, DANCE!"

Our little dog stood up on her hind legs and began to step around in a circle, holding her front paws delicately in front of her. Jeanne held the hoop toward her, down low, and Lady stepped through and lay down. The children clapped and laughed, and Jeanne bowed. When she straightened up, her hands were steady and she was really smiling.

Jeanne (circa *1935*) *Photo courtesy of Denice Hanke*

3

The Playhouse

One evening in early summer three men came to the house to talk to our dad, so I took them to our playroom, where he had his desk. Then I sat down again on the stairs to wait for Grandma to take my younger sister Gwen and me up to bed. That's how I happened to overhear an important conversation.

"Jim, all three of us owe a good amount to the store," I heard one man say.

"Nineteen thirty-three has not been a good year for carpenters," another one added.

"Or for storekeepers." Daddy sort of laughed when he said this, but it didn't sound that funny to me.

"Jim, we know you'd rather have the money," said the first man, "but since we don't have it, we were wondering whether we could build you something in exchange."

"Like an addition to your house or something." This was a new voice, one that sounded kind of shy. "Anything you need, a shed, anything."

"Well, this sounds very interesting. You're right, Mr. Bailey and I would prefer the money that is owed to the store, but perhaps we can work something out." Our dad sounded patient as usual. And kind. "Actually, we do have some lumber left from a job at the store. I'll talk to him and see what he thinks."

Just then Grandma and Gwen came to the bottom of the steps, and I went upstairs with them. In a couple minutes I heard the front door open and shut, and I didn't think of the conversation again for a long time, a month anyway. That's when we got back from our three-week vacation at Uncle Jim and Aunt Gertie's.

Dad parked the car at the front of the house and casually remarked, "There's something in the backyard I think you'll like, girls." Of course we raced around the house, our older sister Jeanne in the lead, and we saw it: the playhouse.

Oh, the squealing with delight and disbelief! You can't imagine what a wonderful little house that was! About ten feet by twelve, white with a shingled roof, a real door knob that turned and latched (we turned it and went in!), two windows that went up and down (we tried them), and—this is really true!—electricity! We flipped the light switch beside the door, and the bare light bulb in the ceiling lit up. It was then that I remembered the evening conversation of a month before.

The playhouse became the center of activity for many of the children in our neighborhood. When Jeanne had her tonsils removed, our parents gave her a special gift, a tiny, single-burner electric stove that went really well with an earlier present of little tin pots and pans. The stove sat on a makeshift counter, a discarded table leaf spanning two wooden orange crates standing on end, and was plugged into an electrical outlet near the door.

We'd be playing in the yard with other kids when someone would get the idea to cook something. So one of us would pick a tomato from the garden while someone else would go in the house and ask Mother for salt and pepper and butter and maybe a couple slices of bread. Jeanne was always the cook, since she was the oldest. After washing the tomato with water from our drinking pitcher, she would bring it into the playhouse, put it in the little pan, and give it a couple of jabs with a knife. We would watch carefully as she added a tiny amount of salt and pepper, sometimes even a little bit of sugar if Mother had sent any. Then we sat on the floor and waited patiently while the tomato heated up, each of us with a small tin cup from our play set.

"It's done. I think it's done," someone would say, probably one of the Shaffer kids.

"Not yet, children," Jeanne would say. "Put your bread in your dishes. It's almost ready." She would add a dab of butter to the tomato and wait just a little longer.

We would break our small sections of bread into pieces and place them in readiness in the little cups. Finally, after more urging, she would pronounce the tomato done and begin ladling it out in miniscule amounts into our miniature bowls. Sometimes we had spoons, sometimes not. Anyway, the tomato would be consumed with great gusto, smacking of lips, and scraping, even licking, of the tiny bowls.

"That was good, Mother," someone would say, and everyone would agree as though we had had a feast.

"Who's going to help with the dishes?" Jeanne would ask, and, surprisingly, there was no scarcity of helpers. Someone was sent to the big house for a basin of soapy water, a dish rag, and a tea towel, and soon the little pot and the tin dishes were back in their places on the rough board that served as a shelf.

As we looked at one another with great satisfaction, someone would invariably say, "Let's do another one."

"Okay," Jeanne would say, "someone go pick a nice tomato," and we'd start all over again.

There was something about the playhouse that made us feel industrious, even those of us who were not normally so, and even other kids in the neighborhood who just showed up to see what was going on. Sometimes two or three days a week we decided to clean the little house. We collected buckets, a basin or two, perhaps a dishpan. We hauled water, rags, soap stuff, vinegar for doing windows, and a scrub brush, all from the kitchen of the big house. Sometimes we scrubbed the old piece of linoleum and vigorously shook the odds and ends of throw rugs. We enjoyed washing the small windows, one child on each side of the glass, making faces at each other and squeaking along with the vinegar solution as we dried the panes. It was so much fun pretending to be a real family doing housework. Sometimes we'd look up and see Mother watching us from the window over the kitchen sink; we'd wave and holler at her and then go back to work in our own house.

One summer morning we had a crew of ten neighborhood kids: two Bensons, Betty and Tootie; five Shaffers, Thelma, Beattie, Lorraine, Danny, and Emory; and three Mugridges, Jeanne, Gwen, and me. We were busy with window-washing, floor-scrubbing, and rug-beating activities. The girls were wearing odds and ends of aprons rescued from our ragbag, since our mothers wore aprons when they were doing any housework. The two little boys were diligently washing the four sleds that were stored in the playhouse during the summer and used for seats or beds. Of course, they had to keep stopping to sit or lie on the sleds or drag them around the yard, but we were having such a good time that nobody fussed at them or told them to get back to work.

We were so engrossed that we didn't notice a strange man come around the back of the big house until he knocked on the open door of the playhouse. No grown-up had ever done that before! We all stopped what we were doing.

"Good morning," he said politely, taking off his hat. He was dressed in a suit and tie, the way all door-to-door salesmen dressed; he seemed to be about the age of our dad. We were too surprised to say anything and just looked at him.

"May I please speak to the lady of the house?" he went on. We looked at each other. He really thought we were a regular house and wanted to try to sell us something! Still not speaking, several of us turned to point at Jeanne.

"How do you do, ma'am?" the salesman asked brightly. Jeanne murmured a nervous hello. "Your neighbor next door thought you might be interested in some of our brushes." He gestured toward our house. Was that Mother at the kitchen window? No, there wasn't anyone there. He opened his case and we crowded around to gaze at his wares. We had all seen these brushes before but always in the house with our mothers.

"What're they all for?" questioned Gwen with interest.

The salesman must have been waiting for this opportunity. "Shoe brushes, scrub brushes, bottle brushes," he pronounced clearly and quickly, pointing them out as he accelerated, "jar brushes, nail brushes, ladies' hair brushes, men's hair brushes, children's brushes, soft baby brushes, suede brushes, pet grooming brushes, brass and copper brushes, AND," he paused, "many, many more!"

We laughed delightedly at his performance while Danny and Emory, the youngest, fell over on the grass in special appreciation. The salesman looked around at his young audience and smiled at them. Danny got to his feet and looked at the collection of brushes. He touched one of them. "We have a little brush like that," he said. "It belonged to my daddy."

"Oh?" questioned the salesman.

"He always cleaned his fingernails with it when he took his bath," explained Thelma.

The younger Shaffers all wanted to add something. "He was a coal miner," chimed in Beattie.

Danny couldn't wait to report the most important fact. "Our

daddy got blowed up in the mine!" They all looked intently at the man to see his reaction.

He was horrified. "Oh, no!" he said, almost in a whisper.

They nodded vigorously and Emory spoke for the first time. "He's dead," the little boy announced matter-of-factly, almost cheerfully. "Ma says he's not coming back."

The salesman cleared his throat. "I'm sorry," he said and paused as though he couldn't think of anything else to say. Then he thought of something. "Would you like a vegetable brush?" The children just looked at him but said nothing. "You could give it to your mother," he added.

They turned to Thelma eagerly. "Is that okay, Thelma? Okay?" She considered the matter for just a second before smiling at the salesman and saying okay. She took the small curved brush he handed her and showed it to her brothers and sisters before remembering to tell him thank you. The others echoed her thanks. The salesman picked up another vegetable brush and held it out to Jeanne.

"This is your gift for looking over my brushes," he went on politely, sounding like a salesman again. "Perhaps at my next visit you'll need something else."

Jeanne must have considered telling him that she was not the lady of the house but simply a child playing with her friends. Then I think she realized that he knew that. "Thank you," she said with dignity and accepted the vegetable brush. The salesman told us goodbye, put on his hat, and went around the side of the house. We waited until he was out of sight to collapse on the grass and burst out in silent laughter.

All of a sudden Jeanne sat up and stopped laughing. "Hey!" she said. "I have an idea!"

We all looked at her with interest. "What? What?!"

"Well," she replied slowly, "we have two vegetable brushes. What should we do with them?"

We all got the idea at the same time and scattered to the garden to find carrots, potatoes, kohlrabi, anything that could be brought back to the little playhouse, scrubbed with vigor, and savored raw, crunched and chewed and digested with all the indescribable, mysterious appetites and seasonings of childhood.

4

Run, Sheepy, Run

The enemy crept closer and closer through the twilight haze.

Suddenly, "Run, sheepy, run!" I shouted, and my sheepy, my team, rose up screaming from behind the bushes in the Buckinghams' backyard and ran. Ran over the grass to Mrs. Cokenour's yard, through her flower beds, across the sidewalk and narrow dirt road, heading for Home, the big catalpa tree that shaded the front of our house and provided the base for many games.

Summer evenings for kids in our neighborhood were usually spent in rigorous games of running, hunting, and chasing while the light changed from rosy sunsets to dusky shadows, always with the admonition from most parents to come home when the street lights came on.

Quite often our favorite game was Run, Sheepy, Run. (Some communities knew this as Run, *Sheep*, Run, but we said *sheepy*.) I loved this game. Here's how it's played: The leader of the first team takes her group over a devious, circuitous path to a hiding place, for example, behind the bushes at the side of the Bensons' chicken coop. The leader then returns to the other group and with a stick draws in the dirt a correct, but misleading, map to where her team is hidden. The second team studies the map then sets out to find the others, whose leader follows along. When the hunters start to get close to the hiding place, the hiders' captain calls out, "Run, sheepy, run!" and she and her team try to get back to the base before being caught.

That evening we had played rather late, racing through streets, around houses and over lawns, shrieking and laughing. After passing Mrs. Cokenour's porch, we heard her screen door slam and were already in the street by the time her angry voice screeched through the night: "Just you wait! I know who you are, and I'm going to talk to your parents in the morning! Not only that, but I'm going to report you to the marshall, and you'll be sent to reform school!"

We were crouched down behind our hedge during her tirade. When she went inside, we stood up and slunk to our homes, not saying much to anyone and going to bed without a protest. In the morning I ate breakfast in a subdued silence, which really annoyed Gwen.

"What'd you do last night?" she asked.

"Just played," I answered between bites.

"Played what?" she persisted.

"Run, Sheepy, Run," I replied. "Just let me eat, will you, Denny?"

"I just wondered," she said. "I thought I heard someone hollering."

I looked at her, not at Mother. Had they heard Mrs. Cokenour's threat? "We were all hollering," I said, trying to be casual. I finished my cereal, helped wash up the dishes, and went outside to sit on the front porch. I was there just a few minutes when I saw Mrs. Cokenour come out of her house across the street. She was carrying her purse, which meant that she was probably going to my dad's store. She came down the steps and walked over to one of the flower beds and shook her head. Some of the flowers were definitely trampled. They looked pretty bad. She didn't see me watching her but just continued down the street and turned the corner in the direction of the store.

My heart sank. She was on her way to talk to my father and the marshall. I was going to reform school.

Before long I was joined by Thelma, Lorraine, and Beattie Shaffer. We sat there for a few minutes without saying anything. Then I said with a sigh, "I guess we might as well make up our minds that we'll be leaving soon. I saw Mrs. Cokenour go to see my dad a little bit ago."

"What do you think it'll be like in reform school?" asked Beattie. We had heard of one boy who lived somewhere across the bridge who had spent some time in reform school, but we had no personal knowledge of the formidable place.

"Do you think they'll beat us?" asked Lorraine.

This was a new thought to me. I had never been beaten, spanked, or even slapped by my parents that I could remember. I swallowed hard and thought about it. "You know, if we do everything right, they wouldn't have any reason to beat us."

"Yeah," agreed Thelma. "We could be really good and do everything they told us."

"Like what?" pressed Lorraine.

"Oh, keep things picked up in your cell, make your bed, do your duties." I couldn't think of more specific things. The other three burst out laughing. "Do your duty" was a phrase they sometimes used in their family to mean "go to the bathroom."

"I know," said Thelma, "prob'ly help with washing clothes and cooking food, stuff like that."

"Don't you think we're kind of young to help cook?" objected Beattie. "I can't lift big kettles."

Lorraine chimed in, "I can't lift clothes baskets, either."

"Well," I said, "they'll find things for us to do that suit our sizes. And you know, we'll have three meals a day."

The Shaffers looked at one another. *Maybe this wouldn't be too bad* was the idea I got from their expressions. I always had three meals; I knew they didn't.

"Do we have to take our own clothes?" asked Beattie. "We don't have a whole lot."

"Oh, no," I assured her, "they'll give us uniforms." Another look passed among them. Suddenly I had an idea. "You know, maybe we could do some good things while we're there."

"Like what?" Thelma sounded uncertain.

"Well, we all go to Sunday School and we know lots of Bible stories," I explained. "We could have little classes and help other girls who've never gone to church."

"Yeah," Thelma said while her sisters nodded in agreement, "like a club." We had never had a club; perhaps our playhouse gang was the closest thing to one. The prospect was appealing.

"Do you think we'll get to march?" asked Beattie. In Vacation Bible School on rainy days we often marched around the church basement to the piano accompaniment of "Marche Militaire" and "Onward Christian Soldiers" and enjoyed it thoroughly.

"I'll bet," I answered. Things were not looking so bad, after all. Then I had another thought. "I wonder," I started, "if maybe we'll have—"

"What? What?" they pressed.

"Bunk beds!" I exclaimed.

"What are bunk beds?" asked Thelma.

"I've never seen any. I've just heard of them," I said.

"What are they?"

"They're beds up on top of beds, like a second layer. It saves room when you have a lot of people," I explained, feeling very knowledgeable.

"How do you get up there?" asked Beattie.

"Ladders!" I answered triumphantly.

"Yeah, ladders, of course," said Thelma.

"Does everybody have their own bed?" asked Lorraine. This was an important question, I knew, because the three girls slept in the same bed. For that matter, most kids I knew slept with brothers or sisters.

"Oh, sure," I replied. Things were getting better and better.

They looked at one another again. "I don't think Ma'll let us go," Beattie had just started to say when Gwen came out on the porch.

"Where you going?" she asked. No one said anything, so she repeated her question. "Ruth, where are you going?"

"Nowhere," I answered.

"I heard you all," she declared. "You're going somewhere. Now, where?"

"All right," I said, "reform school, and you can't go!"

"If you go, I can go!"

"No, you can't! You're not old enough!" For some reason I didn't want Gwen to go with us, though ordinarily we got along very well.

"I'm as old as her!" she announced, pointing at Beattie.

"But you didn't do anything wrong!"

That didn't matter to her. "I don't care. I'm going to tell Mother and she'll make you take me. You'll see!" The screen door slammed as she went back into the house. We heard her yelling for Mother, and I sighed in exasperation. Who knows what will happen now, I thought.

Sure enough, Mother came to the door and spoke through the screen. "Ruth, what is Gwen talking about? Where are you going?"

When I didn't answer right away, Thelma felt that she had to. "Mrs. Mugridge, they're sending us to reform school." Her sisters nodded. "All of us. Ruth, too."

Mother opened the door and came out. "Why would they do that?" she asked. "Who, anyway?"

I decided to confess. "Mother, we ran over Mrs. Cokenour's flowers and ruined them. She said she was going to tell the marshall and he would send us to reform school. She really means it."

"Yeah!" chorused the Shaffers. "She means it!"

"Well," said Mother, "look who's coming down the street with her groceries." We turned to look, and there was Mrs. Cokenour. "I just think I'll go have a little talk with her." Mother went down the steps and across the street. She didn't seem afraid at all; in fact, she put her hand on her neighbor's arm, and from the look on Mrs. Cokenour's face, was speaking very pleasantly. What could there be to smile about, much less laugh?

After a couple of minutes Mother returned to the porch. She took her time coming up the steps, crossing to the swing, and sitting down. She still didn't say anything so I went over and sat down beside her. As soon as I did, Gwen got up and went over to sit on the other side, ignoring the fact that I was glaring at her.

"Mother," I said, "what did she say? Was she mean about it? Is she going to send us to reform school?"

"Girls, I want you to go over to Mrs. Cokenour's yard and look at the flowers that were trampled, and I think you'll understand why she's upset."

"Aw, Mother! Do we have to?" I pleaded. "She's still out there, and she'll yell at us again."

"Yeah, Mrs. Mugridge, she will," said Thelma, sounding even more earnest than I did. Her sisters nodded.

"Are you more afraid of Mrs. Cokenour than you are of reform school?" Mother asked. We didn't know what to say. Mother got off the swing and urged us to the steps. "Just go over and talk to her and look at her flowers. That's all she wants."

"That's what's she tells *you*," I grumbled but went down the steps anyway, followed by the Shaffer girls and Gwen. When I realized that Gwen intended to accompany us, I turned around. "Mother!" I complained.

"Gwen, come up here with me," she said calmly.

"I just thought I'd go with them," Gwen protested. "I wasn't going to say anything." However, she went back up on the porch and sat down on the swing.

The Shaffers and I dragged ourselves across the street and into the yard where Mrs. Cokenour was kneeling by a bed of petunias. I guess she didn't hear me when I cleared my throat, since she didn't look up until I spoke.

"Mrs. Cokenour?" Was she being slow on purpose?

"Oh, Ruth, I didn't hear you. And Thelma? Is that right?" She looked at each of us closely as she spoke. Thelma nodded and Mrs. Cokenour went on. "Are these your sisters, Thelma?" Another nod. "What are your names?"

When her sisters didn't answer, Thelma spoke, "That's Beattie. That's Lorraine."

"How do you do, girls?" Beattie and Lorraine were speechless at being addressed so formally. Mrs. Cokenour smiled at them (Was she playing that she was friendly to catch us off guard?) and said, "I see you playing outside with your little brothers and sister. What are their names?" (Why did she want to know people's names?)

I was surprised to hear Lorraine, the younger, reply, "Danny and Emory and Cacky."

"Catherine," Beattie corrected her sister. "Her real name is Catherine. Our ma wants us to stop calling her Cacky."

"That's probably a good idea, girls," said Mrs. Cokenour seriously. "Besides, Catherine is such a beautiful name."

There was a quick intake of breath from all three girls, and Thelma hurried to explain. "That's our mother's name. Her middle name. Edna Catherine. So that's our little sister's name, too."

I wondered when we were going to get down to business. Mrs. Cokenour must have sensed this, for she changed the subject. "What were you playing last night, girls? You seemed to be having so much fun."

We spoke in one voice, "Run, Sheepy, Run!"

"Oh, I used to play that with my brothers and sisters! I loved that game! There were six of us, so we could play even when no one else was around."

We looked at her, amazed. "That's the same with us!" I exclaimed. "Both our families have six kids!"

"What time do you usually have to go in at night?" she asked.

Again we answered in unison, "When the street lights go on!"

"It's hard to stop playing when you're having so much fun, isn't it?" she remarked.

I couldn't believe she understood that, she was so old. We nodded, not knowing what to say, but we were even more astonished as she went on. "Do you know why I wanted to talk to you?"

Thelma and I looked at each other. I figured that one of us had to say it, so I went ahead, "To tell us we have to go to reform school."

She leaned forward, putting her face in her hands. Was she laughing or crying? We waited. When she finally looked up, I still couldn't tell.

"Girls, I want to apologize," she started. Beattie and Lorraine looked confused, so she began again, "I'm sorry I screamed at you last night and said that stupid thing about reform school. I can't believe I said that."

She looked so miserable that I felt I had to comfort her. "Oh, no, Mrs. Cokenour! We were really bad to run over your flowers like that. You couldn't put up with that, could she, Thelma?" Thelma and her sisters shook their heads.

Six-year-old Lorraine repeated, "We were really bad," and her seven-year-old sister added, "You couldn't put up with that."

Mrs. Cokenour suddenly laughed and said, "Oh, girls, don't make excuses for me. I forgot what it was like to play Run, Sheepy, Run in the evening when it was getting dark and someone was chasing you, and you just had to run and run and run…"

"Yeah," we said. And scream and holler and fall over laughing, it was so much fun, I thought.

"So let's forget what I said about reform school, all right?" she asked.

"Okay," we said.

"But," she went on, sounding stern, "You're going to have to pay for what you've done to my poor little petunias." From the nice way she had been talking, this was quite unexpected.

"We don't have any money, Mrs. Cokenour," Thelma said bravely.

And then, would you believe it, our neighbor changed back to being nice once more. "There, I've scared you again," she said with a laugh. "Here's what I was wondering: Would you help me move my petunias over by the house? That way, people can run across the yard without worrying about the flowers. What do you think?"

We looked at one another and kind of shrugged okay. I glanced across the street and saw Mother on the porch watching, so I waved at her and she waved back. Of course, Gwen did, too. Mrs. Cokenour put her hands down on the ground and pushed herself to her feet. "I'll go get some things to dig with, and we'll do this right away if that's okay with you girls." She went into the house and we just stood there.

"Well," said Thelma, "I guess we're not going to reform school after all."

"Guess not," I answered. "It's probably better this way. Our families would really miss us."

"Yeah," said Beattie, "besides, other than the bunk beds, I didn't think reform school sounded that great anyway."

5

Speaking My Piece

"Well, children, here's Mrs. Ormston with your recitations for Children's Day," announced my Sunday School teacher.

This was no surprise to me. I had watched her making her way around the church basement, stopping at tables where the different classes sat, and handing out papers with our recitations, which we called "pieces." Several of my third-grade classmates groaned as she approached; I was not one of them.

When Mrs. Ormston got to my class, she must have been feeling harassed and peevish. Maybe some of the children had rejected the pieces selected for them as being too long, too hard, or having words that were too big; she probably had had to exchange a number of them. Anyway, without taking much time to match us up with poems, she simply passed out the slips of paper to each of us and told us to come to practice at ten on Saturday. She had turned to leave our table to head to another class when I spoke up.

"Mrs. Ormston, could I have a different piece?"

"Why?" she snapped. "Is this too hard for you?"

I was surprised at her tone, but then I thought, She doesn't know us very well. She and Reverend Ormston haven't been here very long, and she doesn't know the kind of pieces I like.

"Too long? Words too big? What's the matter?" she asked.

"I'd like to pick my own," I explained. She barely controlled a look of exasperation and held out the book. I glanced at the page she showed me and turned to the next page.

"Those are all longer and harder," she said. "Most of the children like the shorter ones."

I pointed at a poem. "I'll take that one if it's okay with you." I tried to be determined. This was important to me.

Mrs. Ormston started to object, "I don't think you'll be able to learn it in the time we have," but my regular teacher interrupted her to say that she thought I would and that this would be a good addition to the program. So that was that. I got the piece I wanted. I *knew* it would be the best.

That afternoon after our Sunday dinner was over, I waited for my father to get settled in his chair. Just as he reached for the newspaper, I spoke up. "Daddy, do you want to read my piece?"

"Sure," he said. "Is it time for Children's Day already?" He glanced at my paper and read the poem rapidly. He didn't ask me whether it was too long or whether I could learn it in time. "Nice," he said. "Very serious. How do you like it?"

"I like it," I answered. "It's kind of sad in a way, but it's different. Would you help me with it like you did last year?"

"Okay," he agreed, "why don't you read it to me?"

I took my paper back, cleared my throat, and started to read:

"Gentle Shepherd, hear my prayer
For little children everywhere.
Dear Lord, I ask you, is it true
You call all children unto you?"

I continued to the end of the poem and waited for him to say something. He just smiled and said, "I think it's going to be really good. Start to memorize it."

"Oh, I already have," I replied.

Several days later, on Wednesday afternoon, the kids in our neighborhood started arriving on our porch. Mother was seated on the swing, her favorite spot, while Beattie Shaffer and her sister Lorraine were showing Mother their pieces. "I get to carry a sand bucket and a shovel," said Beattie, quite pleased. She didn't actually own any, but her Sunday School teacher was going to let her borrow some for the program. Lorraine was going to be in the same set. Her prop was to be a piece of chalk, as used for sidewalk games like hopscotch. They were going to be part of a group of children whose poems celebrated the fun of summer.

"Chalk's no fun," complained Lorraine. She suspected that the sand pail was somehow a better toy than the chalk. Their little brothers, Danny and Emory, were not going to speak but would sing in the children's chorus, so they had to learn the songs.

Their oldest sister, Thelma, who was about my age, had a poem that was eight lines long; it was about liking to go to Sunday School and reading stories from the Bible. My younger sister, Gwen, had a four-line piece about finding pansies with sweet little faces. She didn't seem to have an opinion one way or the other about the lines she had to learn. There were a few other children who came to our front porch tutoring sessions irregularly, but the Shaffer kids were always there. While Mother listened to each child read and helped her pronounce and memorize, the rest played with paper dolls or colored pictures, the words of the pieces providing a pleasant background. We'd look up now and then, listening absently.

I was the last to practice. Instead of reading from the paper, I handed it to Mother. "You can tell me the words if I don't know them."

Thelma looked surprised. "Do you know the whole thing already?"

"Sorta," I fibbed, "but not very well." I let Mother prompt me now and then as I spoke the lines of my piece so that it wouldn't seem as though I were showing off. After I got started, I saw Thelma look up from the paper doll she was dressing. I could tell she was really interested in the way I was saying the poem.

"You like to learn poems, don't you?" she asked me when I finished.

"Yeah," I answered.

"What's your favorite one?

I didn't hesitate. "You remember the poem by Robert Louis Stevenson we had to learn last year in school? 'Where Go the Boats?' I like that."

"Yeah," Thelma agreed, "I like that, too."

"You know, I still say it now and then. Sometimes I can't decide if I like that one better or my new one."

"I like your new one better. It has a good meaning," said Thelma.

"I like to say poems that have a lot of feeling." I elaborated, "I like to play sad or mad or scared, you know what I mean." Then I laughed. "My dad says sometimes I overdo it." I thought for a minute. "Your piece is nice, too."

She shrugged. "It's okay," she said. The next afternoon that we practiced on the porch, Thelma knew her poem without any prompting from Mother.

At the Saturday rehearsals Mrs. Ormston had her patience stretched to the limit. Some of the grade school children had to take care of their preschool siblings, so the sensible thing was to have them sing in the children's chorus. Sensible on the surface, that is. Little kids who haven't been exposed to group discipline often are quite resistant to being moved here and there or arranged in rows or marched in lines beside other children they may or may not know.

The first two rehearsals, in addition to having the grade school children practice their pieces, focused on making sure everyone knew the three songs: "Jesus Wants Me for a Sunbeam," "Jesus Loves the Little Children," and the perennial favorite, "Jesus Loves Me." Regulars at Sunday School knew these already, but at least ten or fifteen children had to be taught.

Poor Mrs. Ormston! At the first rehearsal she thought she could sit at the piano, give the kids a nod, and simply play the accompaniment. Did she ever receive a revelation! First, she went over the words of the first chorus of the Sunbeam song and had the children speak them. So far, so good. Then she sat down at the piano and struck a chord. "All right, now, boys and girls, sing!" She began to play and sing loudly, and then realized that most of the children were not singing but were snickering, then laughing uproariously. She spun around on the piano stool, ready to scold the guilty ones. By that time it was everyone.

Billy Walker's little dog, Buddy, some kind of terrier, had wandered in the open door of the church and up the aisle to the front rows where the children were. Billy's older sister, Jenny, who was seated on the aisle, looked down just as Buddy trotted past and lunged for him. He skittered away from her and ran straight up the steps toward the altar. "Buddy!" Jenny hissed, and chased after him. He dodged and circled the platform, almost gleefully, it seemed.

And now, Billy stood up and joined the fracas from the front row. "Buddy!" he yelled. "Here, Buddy!"

Hearing his master's voice, Buddy suddenly changed course and raced for Billy. He leaped the steps into Billy's arms with such force that he knocked the five-year-old child backward, causing him to sprawl over the legs of Emory and Danny Shaffer, who started to holler and thrash around. Buddy, of course, loved this commotion and joined right in, yipping and scrambling on the boys. Poor Mrs. Ormston stood there shouting, "Children! Children!" but nobody paid any attention to her.

Finally, Jenny Walker managed to pick up the dog and get her little brother settled in his seat again; she then took Buddy to the door, put him out, and quickly shut the door before he could get back in. Thelma Shaffer quieted her little brothers by sitting between them with an arm around each one, exerting a firm, subtle presence. She took care of them so much that, even though she was only eight, they knew when she meant business. Mrs. Ormston, although somewhat disconcerted by the interruption, settled down at the piano once more, and after an introductory phrase, attacked the Sunbeam song with spirit, and we were happy to join in. We sailed through "Jesus Loves the Little Children" and "Jesus Loves Me" because we sang them every Sunday. Mrs. Ormston got to feeling pretty optimistic at this point.

Then we started practicing our pieces.

Our teacher's little five-year-old granddaughter, Lucy, was to open the program with a welcome:

I may be little, but I can say
A great big WELCOME on Children's Day!

Probably her mother and grandmother were more enthusiastic about her being in the program and delivering the welcome than she was, for she refused to say anything for the first two rehearsals. At the last rehearsal she stomped up to the platform, shouted the lines, then held out her hand and demanded, "Where's my gumdrop? "

Her mother said firmly, "Not until you say it nicely."

Lucy repeated the lines in a sugary tone and then held out her hand. "Okay?"

"You didn't hold out your hands like we taught you," said her mother. "You know, on the word 'welcome.'"

Lucy then repeated the lines with an expansive gesture but forgot the sweetness.

"No," started her mother, but four or five kids raised their hands and interrupted with "I'll do it!" "Let me do it!" At this Lucy burst into tears and ran down from the platform, crying noisily. Her mother gave her a gumdrop to stop the howling, and we skipped on to the next speaker.

When my turn came to speak my piece near the end, I got started, but Mrs. Ormston interrupted me with a suggestion. "Ruth, since this is a prayer, why don't you close your eyes and clasp your hands as though you're praying?"

I closed my eyed and clasped my hands momentarily, but after a few seconds, I opened my eyes and put my hands down. "If you don't mind, Mrs. Ormston, that just doesn't feel right," I tried to explain. "I like to look at people when I'm speaking my piece."

"All right," Mrs. Ormston sighed. "It was only an idea. Go ahead, Ruth, you're the last one."

I think that rehearsal was probably my best. The teachers and other kids seemed to listen really well, even the little ones. I couldn't wait till Sunday evening.

Finally, Children's Day arrived, bright, sunny, and perfect. In Sunday School we practiced our songs, and some children went over their recitations if they were still not certain of them. The kids who were in the group called Summer Fun practiced with their props: shovel and pail, chalk, inner tube, bat and ball, jump rope, fishing pole, and picnic basket. Several had to be dissuaded from taking their props home to play with. They were sure to be lost or forgotten, the teachers insisted.

After dinner I asked Mother and Daddy whether they'd listen to me one last time, so they sat down on the sofa. What kind, long-suffering parents! They had heard the poem fifty times, yet they would listen once again just to please me. As usual, Mother's lips moved silently as I spoke the words, while Daddy's eyes glistened slightly.

"I think you'll do okay," he said when I'd finished. "Just remember, don't overact. Be sincere."

Mother nodded. "Don't worry about it," she added. "You know it so well."

I read a book the rest of the afternoon, had a quick meal, changed back into my Sunday dress, wiped my face, combed my hair, and at last was out the door with Gwen. The Shaffers had just passed our house, and we caught up with them. Their clothes were not new but looked freshly washed and pressed; the kids themselves looked scrubbed and rosy.

"I had a bath," reported Danny.

"I did, too," said Emory.

"We all did," announced Beattie.

"You look nice," I said politely.

"You do, too," replied Thelma. We hooked little fingers in a friendly way and walked the short distance to the church, joining in the silly chatter of our younger brothers and sisters.

When we entered the church, we stopped in wonder. The front of the sanctuary was filled with flowers, everything the teachers' gardens could supply. We were assembled in an adjacent room where we practiced our songs quietly as the church rapidly filled with the audience of families and friends. Mrs. Ormston looked in and said, "When you hear the music, come into the sanctuary and go up on the platform for the first song." Her voice sounded a little nervous, but she smiled anyway and went out to start the music.

At the first chord we were ready to go. The third row, made up of the tallest kids, filed in and went up the steps and across the back, followed by the row of middle-sized kids. The smallest children, bunched up in the rear momentarily, took the opportunity to annoy each other with little pinches and tweaks. Fortunately, one of the teachers separated two of the worst before anything serious could break out, and the line started to move up the steps and across the front. Danny Shaffer, mesmerized by the crowd, suddenly saw his mother and stopped.

"Hi, Ma!" he called out, and the rest of the line ran into him. "Hey," he hollered, "quit it!" He glared at the boy behind him, ready, it seemed, for fisticuffs. One of the teachers sprang into action. She grabbed his arm and moved him quickly to his place.

She turned to the audience and spoke cheerfully. "We're going to start our program by singing "Jesus Wants Me for a Sunbeam." She stepped off to the side.

Danny was not finished. "I don't want to be no sun bean," he announced. Mrs. Ormston ignored him and gave a resounding chord, and we all responded heartily:

"Jesus wants me for a sunbeam
To shine for Him each day,
In every way try to please Him
At school, at home, at play.

"A sunbeam, a sunbeam,
Jesus wants me for a sunbeam.
A sunbeam, a sunbeam,
I'll be a sunbeam for Him."

After a couple more verses and choruses our opening number was over, and the audience was applauding enthusiastically. Our teacher,

Mrs. Springer, announced from the side, with some trepidation, I'm sure, "Lucy will now present our official welcome."

To our surprise, Lucy, dressed like Shirley Temple, stepped forward and spoke sweetly, gestured appropriately, and returned to her place. As the brief applause died out, two boys' voices, disguised as those of little girls', piped up, "Where's my gumdrop?" We gasped. Would Lucy go into a tantrum?

Suddenly, Lucy laughed out loud and pointed to her mother in the front row on the side. Her mother stood up and held up a brown paper bag. "After the program," she called out, "gumdrops for everyone!"

We clapped and cheered. Having candy even as simple as a gumdrop was not an everyday occurrence. It seemed my heart would overflow with goodwill toward everyone.

Another child spoke her piece. We sang our second song, "Jesus Loves the Little Children," and walked back to our seats. The Summer Fun group performed almost without incident, except for Freddie Jones tripping over his inner tube. However, he got up immediately and went on with his part.

Next on the program was my sister Gwen. She walked up to the platform in a cute little red dress that Sister had made out of a yard of material just the day before. Her black, shoulder-length hair had been coaxed into bouncy curls by Mother, using long strips of rags. She stood at the assigned spot and smiled down at us, at me in particular, I thought, and I smiled back. She started to speak:

"Gentle Shepherd, hear my prayer
For little children everywhere."

I couldn't believe it. She was saying my piece! I looked across the aisle to where our parents were sitting. I don't think they realized it yet. Gwen continued calmly:

"Dear Lord, I ask you, is it true
You call all children unto you?"

And she walked off the platform and came to sit down in the second row, just in front of me. She turned around and looked at me. "Ruth," she whispered, "did I do okay?" I didn't have the heart to go into it right then. She didn't even know what she had done. I nodded at her and smiled weakly; satisfied, she turned around. It wouldn't be long now, I thought. There's another group of twelve kids who spell out Children's Day ("C is for CHILDREN at Sunday School, who learn to know the Golden Rule"), then Thelma Shaffer, Tootie Benson, and finally me.

The Children's Day group performed very well, except for one kid who held his card with the E upside down. And then it was Thelma Shaffer's turn.

She walked up to the platform and turned to face the audience. Her one good dress was faded but clean; her dark hair was cut short like mine for summer. She looks scared, I thought, as though she can't remember her first words. "I like to go to Sunday School," I started to mouth for her, but she had already begun:

"Gentle Shepherd, hear my prayer
For little children everywhere."

My mouth fell open. This couldn't be happening. Gwen was bad enough, but now Thelma! Was *she* going to stop after the fourth line, too?

"Dear Lord, I ask you, is it true
You call all children unto you?"

No, she was going on!

"Do you know us all by name?
Do you love us all the same?"

I noticed children turning around to look at me, probably wondering what I was thinking, what I was going to do. I closed my mouth, clenched my teeth, and tried not to look at them, just at Thelma.

"Do you care when we are cold
Or when our clothes are worn and old,
When all that we can do is weep,
Too hungry, Lord, to go to sleep?"

There's something funny here, I thought. In a way she sounds like me, the way Daddy taught me, not to be sing-songy, to speak clearly and slowly, to emphasize certain words, but there's a difference. What is it?

"Do all children have the right
To live in laughter, hope, and light?
Free from sickness, hate, and fears
Free from poverty and tears?"

I know what it is, I thought. I am good at being dramatic, and she isn't. She is very...simple and plain. (Was I hunting for the word *sincere*...or *real*?) As I listened and heard her speak...so simply and plainly...of poverty and tears, I felt a twisting hurt in my chest. There was not a sound anywhere in the church, not even kids whispering or wooden pews creaking. I glanced sideways to where the grownups were sitting. My own father was wiping a tear from his cheek. I heard him clear his throat softly, a sure sign that he was moved.

"Lord, teach our world somehow to find
A way to be like you, more kind;
A world that helps us when we try
To save our dreams before they die.
This is the prayer, O Lord, I make
In your name, for children's sake. Amen."

What should I do? I thought. I'm not going to say the whole darn thing over again, that's for sure.

Tootie Benson went up to say her piece. It was eight lines of something, I don't remember what. She finished and returned to her seat, and I got up and walked to the front. Suddenly I knew what I was going to do. I turned to face the audience and looked down at my parents, whose expressions were hard to read, but I thought I caught a glimpse of...what? curiosity? sympathy?

"'Where Go the Boats?'" I announced, and I saw my mother glance quickly at my father.

"Dark brown is the river,
Golden is the sand.
It goes along for ever
With trees on either hand.

Green leaves a-floating,
Castles of the foam,
Boats of mine a-boating—
Where will all come home?

On goes the river
And out past the mill,
Away down the valley,
Away down the hill.

Away down the river,
A hundred miles or more,
Other little children
Shall bring my boats ashore."

I was the last child to speak. The rest of the kids came up on the platform to sing "Jesus Loves Me," and as we jostled into lines, Thelma ended up next to me. While we sang, I didn't look at her, but our hands accidentally touched. I was still upset, but somehow our little fingers hooked. I glanced over at my parents and caught Daddy's eye, and he gave me a little nod. Then the audience joined in on the chorus, and after that, the Children's Day celebration was over.

Except for the gumdrops, of course.

6

Butcher Hole

"What's the buckets for?" asked Danny.

"You'll see," I told him.

Everyone had met in front of our house as usual to go swimming down at Butcher Hole. We wore our bathing suits and carried old, worn-out towels. No one we knew had beach towels. In fact, not everyone was even wearing a regular bathing suit. The Shaffer kids usually just wore old clothes. The suits the rest of us wore were all hand-me-downs, woolen with moth holes, and shrunken sizes smaller than they were originally. But as kids growing up in the Depression, no one cared what we wore.

We started down our little street to the river, a straggling bunch of kids all set for an afternoon of fun. In addition to Gwen and me, there were eight others: Thelma Shaffer and her five younger brothers and sisters, even Cacky, who was about a year old; and Betty Benson and her sister Tootie. Thelma, Betty, and I were carrying old buckets in addition to other stuff.

"We got the best swimming hole in town," declared Betty, and everyone agreed.

"Yeah!"

"Better'n Otts' Dam," chimed in Beattie.

"Yeah," we responded again, almost like a litany.

"Better'n that ol' Blue Hole!" hollered Danny.

"That's right!" I yelled, and everyone cheered.

Then we started chanting our name poem, a rhythmic listing of all of us kids. I had created an interesting way to combine our names that was lots of fun:

"Thelma, Beattie, Betty, Tootie,
Danny, Denny, Rainey, Ruthie,
Em'ry Dick, and Baby Caa-cky!"

(I had had to use Emory's middle name to make the rhythm come out right.) All the kids liked it and repeated it over and over, a tuneless refrain that somehow gave us noisy pleasure in our own company. Someone would decide to change the order; for instance, "Thelma, *Betty,* Beattie, Tootie" or "Thelma, Betty, *Tootie,* Beattie," and it would strike us so funny that we'd have to stop and laugh. Even Cacky, bumping along in the rusty wagon pulled by one of her brothers or sisters, chortled happily. This is how we made our way along the gravel road to the top of the slight grade leading down to Butcher Hole.

We ran down and dumped our things off in a clump of grass. Gwen and I took off our shoes as did Betty and Tootie; the Shaffers didn't wear any in the summer, so they didn't have to bother. They were the first of our gang to splash into the water, and they stood there shivering while Thelma barked out her rules and threats.

"No fightin'! No goin' off where I can't see you! Danny! Emory! No gettin' off the first ledge or you're goin' home! When I call you, you better come! You got that?" Thelma sounded meaner than she was, and her brothers and sisters listened to her as well as could be expected. They sometimes whined and complained but actually didn't behave too badly. They knew that if Thelma told on them, none of them could go anywhere.

"Can we play with the buckets?" asked Emory.

"No! They're for something else," Thelma said sternly. "We'll tell you when it's time."

"Why not now?" wheedled Danny.

"It's not time," she said with finality. "Mind now, don't go off that first ledge."

Actually, I thought she was a little strict with the boys about that. One of the things that made Butcher Hole unique was the random, natural placement of large flat rocks throughout the riverbed, creating smooth ledges of varied heights and, therefore, depths of water. People who often swam there knew exactly where the ledges were; it was fun stepping off a slab of rock where the water reached your knees, as on the first ledge, into a spot with the water up to your waist, second ledge; or to your shoulders or even over you head, third ledge. We were proud of the smoothness of the riverbed rocks, even though newcomers were occasionally startled by unexpected drop-offs.

Thelma settled at the river's edge with Cacky, who was satisfied to play with a small rubber doll and pat her hands in the water. Thelma dribbled streams of water over the baby's head to make her laugh and glanced around constantly to check on her brothers and sisters. The two little boys were lying in the shallow water, blowing bubbles and trying to hold their breath. Beattie and Lorraine, or Rainey, as the younger ones called her, were playing a game with Tootie and Gwen that involved holding hands, jumping around in a circle, and suddenly dropping off the first ledge with a lot of splashing and squealing.

Betty and I went into the water for a bit, then came out and sat down on a little grassy spot that gave us a good view of the whole swimming area. On the other bank were five kids we didn't know. First, they swam in the deep section, then climbed up on the big flat rocks on the opposite shore to lie in the sun. Two other boys in inner tubes (pronounced *enner* tubes in our area) were floating around, kicking and pushing at each other. I couldn't take my eyes off those boys. I loved inner tubes. Our family never seemed to have any; I don't know why. My fascination extended to other inflatable rubber toys, but I never asked my parents for one because of an embarrassing incident two years before, the summer our sister Jeanne had St. Vitus' Dance.

In late August before school started, since Jeanne had almost fully recovered from her strange disease, our family decided to go to Crystal Beach near Johnstown for a picnic. We had parked in the shade near the picnic tables and spread a blanket for Jeanne. Bobby helped Mother and Daddy with getting our lunch ready, and John went with Gwen and me to the beach with instructions to return in half an hour.

Our brother John was so much fun in the water. He let us ride on his back while he swam underwater. He stooped down so that we could climb up on his shoulders, and he'd throw us off and then grab us quickly before we were under the water too long. He let me slide down the big sliding board and caught me at the bottom where it was deep. He was helping Gwen to float when I noticed the girl with the gray and red rubber inflatable horse.

She was a little older than I and was playing by herself, struggling to make the horse stay upright while she mounted it. Finally, she gave up and just threw herself across the horse's back and paddled around, kicking her feet. In a little while a woman came along and called the girl, telling her it was time to go eat. After a few last kicks the girl simply walked out of the water and left the horse floating by itself. I stood there watching it for a few minutes until John called to me that it was time to go back to the picnic area.

"Okay, I just want to play a little longer," I told him. He stood there and looked at me for a few seconds and then put Gwen on his shoulders and walked up onto the beach. He hesitated at the edge of the water.

"All right, but don't go out in deep water," he said reluctantly and left the beach with Gwen.

I didn't waste any time. I took the horse into shallow water and mounted it; I walked and pushed my way into deeper water where I could float. I paddled around for a minute or so before heading back toward low water, remembering what John had said. I lay across the horse and kicked and splashed. I imagined what it would be like to play with the beautiful red and gray horse at Butcher Hole with the other kids all around, admiring it and asking for a turn.

A man walking along the beach stopped and smiled. "Boy, you're having a lot of fun all by yourself, aren't you?"

I ignored his question. "Whose horse is this?" I asked. "Is it yours?"

"Oh, my, no," he answered. "It's for anyone who wants to play on it. Have a good time," and he walked on.

I thought about it briefly and then let the air out of the horse. I folded it up as compactly as I could, left the water, and headed toward the picnic area. When I got close, I saw that one of our car doors was open. I pushed the flattened horse under the back seat as far as it would go and joined my family at the table. We had a really good lunch of baked beans, city chicken, potato salad, and cake. Afterward, I was resting with Jeanne on the blanket when I heard Daddy say, "What's this thing?" I sat up and saw him at the car door, shaking out the inflatable horse. "Where'd this come from?"

John came around the car and looked at the thing our dad was holding. "Hey!" he said. "That's the horse from down at the beach!" He turned to me. "I saw you looking at that horse. Did you bring it up here?" I didn't say anything.

"Ruth," asked Daddy, "did you bring this horse up here and put it in the car?" I nodded slowly. "Why did you do that? It doesn't belong to you."

"The man said it didn't belong to anyone," I tried to defend myself. "He said anyone could have it."

"He meant anyone could *play* with it, but it belongs to the park," explained my father. "You'll have to take it back."

I looked to my mother for help, but she just repeated what my father had said. "You'll have to take it back, Ruth."

I picked up the horse but just stood there until Bobby spoke up. "I'll go with you."

"I will, too," said Jeanne, getting up from the blanket.

"Me, too," chimed in Denny, not wanting to be left out of anything.

"Oh, well, I may as well go, too," said John, pretending to groan, so we all made our way down to the beach, with me carrying the deflated horse. I was glad they went with me, but I had to put up with a lot of teasing for a long time.

So now I sat with Betty on the shore and watched the inner tube boys, paddling with one hand and spinning around in circles. I couldn't understand it. We had a car and the store had a truck. Why weren't there any inner tubes lying around? Just then Betty touched me on the arm and pointed to the other side where the kids were leaving, picking their way across the rocks at the edge and jumping up on the bank. At almost the same time the two other boys decided to leave the water, their rubber tubes slung over their shoulders. We waited while they put their shoes on, picked up their towels and passed us on their way up the little hill to the road. Finally! We looked at each other and smiled. Our wonderful adventure was about to begin!

About a week before, Betty and I had noticed unusual activity on the other side, bursts of laughter and screaming coming from behind the trees and bushes along the steep hillside, followed by kids bursting out into the open, running and jumping into the deep water on their side of the river. I asked Bobby if he knew what was going on over there.

"Oh, yeah," he said, smiling. "They're sliding down the clay path."

"What's that?" I asked.

"Well," he explained, "you know that whole hill over there has a lot of clay all through it, and there are two paths." I *didn't* know that. "There's the walking path the kids use most of the time. It's real steep. Then there's the other one. It goes more sideways, not so steep. Anyway, some years they don't use it at all, and it gets all overgrown. They must have cleared it off to be able to slide 'cause it has to be real smooth, no sharp roots or rocks or anything."

"What do they slide on, sleds?" Betty wondered.

Bob grinned. "Their hind ends, what else?" I almost gasped. *Hind end,* to us, was one word, *hineden,* and a halfway dirty one at that. I decided not to say anything, since I wanted to find out more about the clay path.

"But what makes it slippery?" I asked. "It's just like dirt, isn't it?"

I think Bob felt important to be able to answer all our questions. "Water, of course. They carry buckets of water up the hill and empty them down the path till it's all soaked." He paused. "Don't think you're going to slide on it, though. Kids on the other side don't like it if we go over there without them being there."

Betty and I hadn't said anything more to my brother about the clay path, but the idea for our escapade had taken hold of both of us, so that when were alone with Thelma, we made our plans. It was to be no small undertaking, since all of the younger children would be involved. Betty and I each had a sister to watch out for, while Thelma could never do anything without her five siblings, including a baby that could hardly walk yet. We decided not to reveal the adventure to anyone until we were actually embarked upon it. And the time was now!

First, we had to coax the kids away from their own games of jumping, splashing, playing baptism, blowing bubbles, and holding their heads under water. Finally, when we told them we were going to cross the river, they became excited and cooperative. We got everybody lined up at the point where the ledges would not be too difficult to navigate nor the water too deep. Well, except for one place where we would have to be careful that no one stepped *down* instead of *across.* We felt sure we would be able to watch everyone and have no problems, since we older ones were all of eight years old.

And so we started across, with Betty and Thelma at the head of the line, Betty carrying a bucket and Thelma carrying Cacky. Betty was to be available to help Thelma in case of any problems with the baby. Then came Tootie and Gwen with a bucket between them, and Beattie and Lorraine with another bucket. After the two little boys, I was to bring up the rear with two buckets. This changed when Danny demanded a bucket and Emory chimed in, so with certain misgivings I gave them one of my buckets.

Everybody concentrated on stepping carefully and holding the buckets out of the water. With Betty guiding her, Thelma, who had a hard time time seeing around the baby, managed to reach the big rocks on the other side without a crisis. Then Betty helped the four squealing little girls, one at a time, to step *over* the dangerous place and not *down into* it. They reached the other side and scrambled up on the rocks; then they turned to watch the progress the boys and I were making.

I had just congratulated myself on our luck in getting ten kids of assorted ages across the river without too much difficulty when it happened. Danny's foot slipped as he tried to step across to the next ledge, and he struggled to keep his balance. When he felt his brother jerking, Emory let go of the bucket and Danny fell into the water. Of course, the pail tilted, filled with water and sank, pulling the astonished Danny with it into water way over his head. I yelled to Emory to stay where he was and hold my bucket, and I jumped in after Danny. He was still under the water when my flailing hands found him and pulled him to the surface, choking and gasping. I thought at first he was going to be mad, his face was so red, but when he stopped coughing, he unexpectedly laughed out loud.

"I almost drownded!" he exploded. "But I didn't lose my bucket!" I realized that he was still holding the handle of the bucket that had almost gotten him drowned in the first place. The other kids were still clapping and hollering when I managed to get him and Emory across the difficult spot and up on the rocks with the rest of them.

While the younger kids looked around at the unfamiliar surroundings, Betty and I filled the five buckets and set them near the path, ready for the next phase of our adventure. We were just about ready to line up the kids for the upward hike when Thelma spoke up. "I ain't going up."

Betty and I looked at her in surprise. After all the work getting the kids across the river, she wasn't going up? "Why?" I asked.

At first she didn't say anything, but then I saw her look down at the baby, who was patting a little pile of damp, gray mud. "I'm afraid something might happen to Cacky," she whispered. "You know, like Danny."

"Danny's okay," said Betty. "He didn't even cry."

"I know," Thelma said firmly. "We'll just wait for you down here."

The kids had become curious at last. "What are we going to do over here?" asked Beattie.

"Yeah," piped up Tootie, "are we going up the hill?"

Danny hadn't forgotten his earlier question. "What's the buckets for?"

Then Gwen's question made me nervous: "Ruth, are we allowed to be over here?"

I wasn't sure about that, but I definitely was not going to admit it. "Nobody told us we *can't* come over here."

Tootie brought us back to our real purpose for being here. "What are we going to do when we get to the top?"

Her sister Betty answered, "You'll see. It'll be fun."

"C'mon, tell us," Tootie coaxed, and the others joined in, "Tell us! Tell us!"

Betty and I looked at each other and decided to give in. "Okay," I said, "we're going to slide down."

They just looked at us. Finally, Gwen spoke for the others. "On what?"

Betty grabbed Gwen's hand and pulled her down the path, the rest of us stumbling after them. She went past a bunch of bushes and pointed up the hill. "On that!" she exclaimed triumphantly. I watched the kids as they gazed up the narrow trail of gray-brown clay, smooth and still slick-looking in the cool shade of the over-hanging branches.

Emory stooped down and sank his small hands in the clay and brought up two damp globs that he squeezed until little curls escaped from between his fingers. "Look, I made wohms," he declared proudly.

Interesting possibilities leaped into my head. "Thelma," I started, "if you're not going up the hill—"

"I know, I know," she broke in. "I just thought of the same thing."

"I'll pour water down at different spots as I go up the hill," I said, thinking out loud, "and then I'll throw the empty buckets down for you."

"Okay," she agreed and placed Cacky near the clay path where she could keep an eye on her. The baby settled happily on the damp ground and began to pat the soft mounds beside her. Betty started the excited kids up the other trail. I followed with a bucket that was full to start with, but with my struggling and slipping, was soon just half-full. After about fifteen or twenty feet I stepped over to the clay trail and poured the water the short distance to the bottom and then let go of the bucket. Thelma caught it and as I watched, began to fill it with clumps of clay.

"Not too much," I called to her. "That clay'll be real heavy." I went back to the other trail and headed down for another bucket of water. Betty and the little kids were taking a rest but were not discouraged by the steepness of the hill. I heard them laughing as they started up again. When I finally brought the fourth bucket up the path, however, Betty and I decided we'd be satisfied with halfway.

"The kids are starting to whine," whispered Betty. "I think we should just slide down from where we are now." I was glad to agree; my legs were really tired. The children, happy not to have to climb any higher, followed me over to the sliding path and watched me pour the last bit of water down the trail, with the empty bucket bumping wildly after it.

Betty took the lead position as planned, sitting down on the smooth, narrow clay pathway, cleared of stones and roots. She dug in her heels and braced herself as one by one the other kids settled in behind her, Tootie, Emory, Beattie, Danny, Lorraine, Gwen, and me. We sat close to each other, hooking our legs around the person in front and hugging as hard as we could. I thought I heard Emory say in a worried voice that he had to pee, but Beattie told him firmly that he had to hold it.

"Let's do our name cheer as we get going," I suggested quickly as we began to inch forward, so the sounds of "Thelma, Beattie, Betty, Tootie" began to ring out down the hill. Betty pulled her feet in and I gave a big push, and slowly, slowly, our little train started to move. Is this all the faster we're going to go, I wondered, a little disappointed, and then all of a sudden we took off. The laughing voices faded out with "Danny, Denny" and began a soaring scream that rose to a shriek as we accelerated. That was the sound that Betty and I had heard from across the creek the week before, exhilarated, frightened, ecstatic.

"Hold on, hold on!" I yelled, for we were really going fast, straight for a bit, then curving around trees and bushes, then straight again, but no one heard me through the noise. The clay was very slippery, a perfect surface for sliding, better than any sliding board

I'd ever tried. I tightened my arms around Gwen, feeling actually afraid for the first time. I felt a sudden sharp burning along the outside of my right leg but didn't dare look to see what it was. I just held on to my sister, wondering whether this adventure was worth it.

Now we could see Thelma at the bottom, holding Cacky and looking up with an excited, fearful expression as her four younger brothers and sisters, plus friends, came flying down the hill toward her. I'm sure she didn't hear me hollering for her to get out of the way, but she moved off to the side anyway as we slid the last couple of yards on the level and came to a stop in a heap, sprawling and exhausted, some laughing, some crying. Betty and I just lay there for a few minutes, relieved that no one was hurt and glad that the whole thing was over with no one dead.

Finally I got up. Thelma had put the baby down and was hugging Emory. "Was it fun?" she asked. "Was it fun, Em'ry?"

He had almost stopped crying but started up again at her question. "I was scared, Selma, I was scared," he whimpered.

Beattie was sympathetic. "But you didn't cry, Buddy! You were a big boy like Danny."

This pleased both boys. "I wasn't scared, Thelma," said Danny, and then to be honest, he added, "'cept maybe a little bit."

Then Beattie remembered. "You can go pee behind that bush now," she told Emory.

He wiped his eyes, smearing clay and tears together. "I don't have to go now," he smiled, his sweet, sunny self once more. "Are we going up again?"

Our resounding "NO!" was deafening, but it made us all laugh. "I'm glad we did it once, though, aren't you?" Betty asked me as we headed back to the creek, carrying the buckets half-filled with the clay that Thelma had dug for us.

"Oh, yeah," I agreed. We organized the kids again, with Betty in the lead, followed by Thelma and the baby, then all the rest, ending up with me at the back. We went into the water, everyone talking happily about our adventure. It was amazing how the younger kids remembered just where the ledges were, *step down, step over, step up, be careful,* and then the last beautiful, flat layer of rock that meant we were on our own safe side again.

It was then that I realized we had left one bucket behind on the other side. There was nothing to do but go back for it, since it belonged to my family. I gave Betty the bucket I had been carrying and went back across the river, a lot faster now that I didn't have to watch out for the little kids. I scrambled over the rocks onto the river bank, went to the clay trail, and retrieved the bucket. I had just passed the walking path when, unexpectedly, several voices accosted me. "Hey! What are you doing over here?"

I had forgotten that I was on unfriendly territory. I was tempted to run, but I was also curious, so I stood still. I turned around and saw two girls about my age, eyeing my bucket of clay with suspicion. "Are you stealing our clay?" demanded one of them.

Stealing their clay? "I thought it was just here…for anyone who wanted it," I explained weakly. Was my wonderful adventure going to end in a fight? I hated the thought of a fight more than just about anything. Maybe I should just dump out the clay and go back to my own side of the river. But first, "Do you own this hill?" I asked, feeling very brave.

"My daddy does," declared the same girl, taking a step closer. Oh, no, I thought. She continued, "And he also owns the bridge and the water that runs under the bridge." I looked at her. She was having a hard time holding her mouth straight, and then she suddenly laughed out loud, the other girl joining in. "I had you going, didn't I?" she giggled.

I was so relieved I couldn't be mad. "Yeah, you did," I admitted, kind of smiling. Then I surprised myself by saying, "You can come over on our side any time you want to. It's okay." Then I added, "My name's Ruth."

The first girl made a weird sound like a yelp. "That's my name, too!" she said. "Isn't that funny?"

"Yeah," I agreed, although I didn't think it was all that funny. Thelma's middle name was Ruth, and across the street was a friend a year older than I whose name was Ruthie Buckingham. She often played with us. I knew a lot of Ruths. I looked at the other girl.

"Millie," she offered. "You can have all the old clay you want. We don't care."

"Thanks," I said, "I have to go now. Come over sometime," and I turned back to the creek and made my way across with the heavy bucket. I put it with the four others at the grassy spot and joined the kids in the water.

Betty was trying to teach Tootie and Gwen to float, while Thelma was giving her brothers and sisters their weekly bath. They had taken off their old, clay-dredged clothes and were soaking them in the water. Cacky was already bathed and was staggering around on the grass, delighted to be naked, dry, and cool. Thelma was seated at the river's edge, ruthlessly scrubbing Danny, who was howling as usual. She soaped the washrag with the cake of Ivory and passed the soap to Beattie and Lorraine, who lathered up each other's hair and then lay back with their heads in the water.

Emory was just sitting on the first ledge, waiting, when the white cake of soap floated by, just out of his reach. I saw him idly watching it but didn't expect him to suddenly lurch after it into deep water. By the time I yelled at him to stop, he had already disappeared under the water, the tempting bar of Ivory dancing away on the waves. He was gone. My friends and I were the only ones on our side of the river, and I was the only who saw what happened. I was about ten, twelve feet away and was not a good swimmer.

"Betty! Betty! Help me! Emory—!" I yelled and threw myself underwater in his direction. After five or six seconds I came up and looked around. Was I even close? I went down again and felt around until all at once, I ran into a body, but before I even surfaced, I was frustrated. It was Betty. "Help me, help me!" I cried. "He's down here somewhere!" We both went under again and almost immediately found his little body, limp and unresisting.

We pulled him up and hugged and shook him, crying his name over and over, but he didn't respond. Betty and I carried him up to the first ledge past Gwen and Tootie, who stood wide-eyed and scared, to the edge of the water where a screaming Thelma met us. She snatched the little boy from us, calling his name and kissing his face. She held him in her arms and started to drag him to the grassy spot.

Danny, unexpectedly furious, charged the two of them, knocking them over practically on top of Cacky, who began bawling indignantly. I couldn't believe it. With all the crying and screaming going on, Danny was pounding Emory, yelling "Quit it! Quit it, Emory! Quit it!" Quit what, I thought impatiently. What we needed was a grownup who would know what to do. I started for the road, but before I went more than two steps, something happened. Something unbelievable.

A funny sound came from Emory's throat as he lay sprawled on the ground partly on top of Cacky and tangled with Thelma. Danny was still kneeling beside him, punching him and hollering, when all of a sudden, a trickle of river water bubbled from between Emory's lips and became a gushing flow, a cup, a quart, I don't know how much. All over Thelma. Emory's eyelids fluttered, and he began to throw up and then to cough and finally, to cry.

We all stood around him, not knowing what to say. Thelma, however, hugged him and, crying herself, kept telling him not to cry. After a minute or so he stopped crying and looked at her. "Selma," he asked solemnly, "are you mad at me?"

"No, no, Emmy!" She tried to keep from blubbering. "Why?"

"I dremp someone was hitting me," he said.

"That was Danny!" hollered the other kids. "That was Danny!"

"*I* was mad at you," Danny admitted. "I thought you was playin' dead."

Emory looked at him with interest. "Didya?"

"Yeah."

"Well, okay, then," said his little brother. Then he thought of something. "I don't have to take my bath now, do I? Can't we just go home?"

His wheedling tone didn't deter Thelma. "Maybe just your head and your ears. You know Ma always checks. Come on down to the water." They got up and went to the water's edge, where Thelma picked up the washrag. "Where's the soap?"

Then I remembered. "It's gone, Thelma. That's what Emory reached for when he went under. It's probably under the bridge by now."

"On its way to Johnstown," put in Gwen. That's what we always said when we dropped things over the bridge into the river.

"Oh, rats," moaned Thelma. "Ma'll kill me. That's the second cake of soap I've lost this summer. You know what Ivory costs." Actually, I didn't. Even though our dad owned the general store in town, I never had to shop and pay for things the way Thelma did.

"I have an idea," offered Betty. "You know, that clay kinda looks like Lava soap. Maybe if you smear it around, it would sorta loosen the dirt."

"I think I'll try it," said Thelma. "It can't hurt." She pulled Emory to her, calling at the same time, "Bring me a hunk of that clay, Danny!" Her little brother ran to the buckets of clay and dug out a little handful and rushed back to Thelma, who smeared a generous amount of the slimy stuff around Emory's neck and ears. Then she wet the washrag and rubbed firmly while Emory squirmed and whimpered in discomfort. She twisted one end of the rag and tried to clean out his ears, but he resisted so strongly that she just gave a final flourish with the cloth and released him. Everyone stood around and surveyed the reddened skin, eventually pronouncing him "prit'near clean." (It was several years before I realized that phrase had started out as "pretty nearly.")

There was nothing to do now but go home. The Shaffer kids dried off and put on clean clothes from the rusty wagon, replacing them with Cacky and their wet things. The rest of us just put our soggy towels around our shoulders and, loaded down with our clothes and four buckets half-filled with wet, heavy clay, headed up the little hill to the road. We took a short cut across Bloughs' back-yard, our little troop somewhat subdued, quite a contrast to the jubilant bunch that had gone to the river a couple of hours earlier. Thelma knew better than to tell her brothers and sisters not to talk about any trouble they had experienced. They always forgot and told anyway.

"There's Ma on the porch," said Beattie. "I'm gonna tell her about the slide." She ran ahead with Lorraine close behind. "Ma, Ma!" she hollered as she ran up the steps. "We went up a big hill and slid all the way down!"

"We had so much fun, Ma!" Lorraine yelled. "I can put my face down in the water!"

"I can, too, Ma!"

"Ma," said Danny, "Ma, I almost drownded, but Ruth pulled me up."

Emory pulled at his mother's sleeve. "I did, too, Ma!" he declared proudly. "We had fun!" Then as an afterthought, "I throwed up, Ma, but I'm okay now."

"Are you clean? Did everyone get a good bath?" asked Mrs. Shaffer, fanning herself with a heavy paper fan, compliments of the funeral home.

"Oh, yeah!" they chorused. She pulled the boys to her and looked in their ears and around the back of their necks. We held our breath while she inspected Emory's reddened skin.

"Okay," she finally said, and the rest of us relaxed. "I'm glad you had a good time." She looked at Thelma. "Did everyone behave? Did they listen to you?"

"Oh, yeah, Ma," Thelma reported, "everyone was real good."

"'Cause you know if they're not, everyone stays home," Mrs. Shaffer declared, unnecessarily. They all knew that.

Cacky let out a squawk for attention, so Thelma picked her up from the wagon and took her up the steps to her mother. "Oh, you little pee-cat, you're all wet!" exclaimed Mrs. Shaffer. "Thelma, take her in and change her." Thelma took the baby from her mother and started through the screen door before looking back.

"I forgot to tell you, Ma. We lost the soap."

"What!" Mrs. Shaffer yelled. "That's the second time this summer! Well, that's it! No swimming tomorrow!"

Nobody said anything, but I thought she was acting kind of mean. Then she glanced over at me. "Ruth," she said with concern, "what on earth did you do to your leg?" Sometimes she sounded nice, like now.

I looked down at my right leg. There was an angry red scratch that stretched from my knee along my outer thigh to the edge of my bathing suit. That's when I remembered the sudden stinging pain I had felt during our glorious slide. "Oh, I guess I scratched it on something when we were sliding down the hill," I said, sort of laughing, trying to sound as though it didn't bother me, but all I could think of was that awful, burning iodine that Mother would insist on painting my leg with. I picked up my two buckets of clay and started after Betty, Tootie, and Gwen, then called back over my shoulder, "Bring your clay over tomorrow. I have an idea about what we can make with it."

I walked the short distance to our house; Gwen had already gone in the side door. "Thelma, Beattie, Betty, Tootie," I spoke softly to myself. There was no one around to hear me. "Danny, Denny, Rainey, Ruthie." I ran up the steps to the side door. "Em'ry Dick and Baby Caa-cky." Pictures, thoughts of the day flashed through my mind: the cheerful, noisy walk to Butcher Hole, our cautious trip across the river, the climb up the steep hill with exhausted kids, and the screaming plummet down the narrow clay path. Grabbing Danny blindly from the water, desperately hunting for Emory, seeing Thelma's anguish as she huddled over the limp body of her little brother. That's what it feels like to have your heart break, I thought, stunned at the revelation. And then, the incredible, indescribable flooding of joy as Emory disgorged the river water and reclaimed his life.

Just before I opened the screen door, I looked down at the buckets of gray-brown clay that I intended to take to the cellar to keep cool and damp. I couldn't help smiling. I could hardly wait till the next day. It was going to be so much fun.

Bob with Lady and me (circa *1932*)

7

The Bleak Midwinter of '35

It was Christmas Eve and I couldn't get to sleep.

Since Uncle Will was living with us at the time, Gwen and I were sleeping in the small bed in Mother and Daddy's room. We had talked quietly for a while, trying to repress our excitement, and then had agreed to try to go to sleep. It worked for her, but I was too keyed up. Besides, there were interesting sounds out in the hallway: footsteps going up to the attic, voices whispering, and *things* softly bumping the walls as they were being carried downstairs. Since most of the tree decorations had been taken down to the living room earlier that day, these *things* were possibly presents.

I heard Mother say to someone, "The WPA men made doll furniture that they were selling for a dollar a piece. I had a choice of beds, cradles, chairs, and rockers, so I picked—"

I held my ears quickly so that I would still be surprised in the morning. When I took my hands down in about a minute, the hallway was quiet again. Maybe next year, or the year after, I thought, I'll be old enough to stay up and help decorate the tree. I had asked Mother about this possibility, and she had just answered, "We'll see." I knew this meant that if I stayed up, Gwen would want to stay up also, and she was just too young, even though she was only twenty months younger.

I thought about all the things I had done that day, starting with an errand I had run for Mother.

"Go to the store and ask your daddy what he's sending for us to have tomorrow, so I can make plans," she told me. This was a common occurrence for me. Quite often our menu depended on what had not been sold in the meat department.

"Tell her it'll probably be a couple of tough old birds that'll be good to cook with noodles," was Daddy's answer when I found him in the produce department, counting oranges into a small basket.

"Waffles would be nice if she feels like making them," he added, "but whatever she wants to do is okay."

"Chicken and noodles and waffles! Sounds good to me," said my brother John, who had just gotten back from making a grocery delivery and was checking in with Dad. I walked with him toward the office, a small raised area in the middle of the store where Romaine worked, sending and receiving money and purchase receipts by means of little cups dancing on overhead wires. John saw me eyeing some items on one counter.

"Last minute shopping?" he asked.

"No," I spoke sadly, "I don't have any money. I wanted to buy something for Denny and Jeanne, but I don't have any money."

"How much do you need?"

"Oh, just a quarter," I answered quickly.

He laughed and pulled out some change from his pocket. "Here's thirty cents," he said, handing me three dimes. "This is for shining my shoes. Have a good time shopping!" And he left to make more deliveries.

"Thank you, John!" I called after him. Oh, it was so wonderful having a grown-up brother of seventeen who had money! I looked at the three dimes and took a deep breath. I turned to the counter again; I knew what I wanted for Jeanne, a small bottle of hand lotion that cost ten cents. It took longer to decide on Gwen's present, but eventually I settled on a book of paper dolls that cost five cents. Fifteen cents left over! I didn't think John would ask for the change, so I bought myself a box of crayons (pronounced *crans* in our area) for ten cents and a coloring book for a nickel. I paid the clerk and floated happily out of the store.

When I got home, I gave Mother the message from my father and went upstairs to hide the presents under the bed before Gwen saw them. I didn't have wrapping paper, but that didn't matter. Fancy paper was a waste of money.

A short time later when I was sweeping the front steps, Thelma Shaffer went by on her way to the drug store for cough medicine. I told her to be sure to go to the Christmas Eve service because all the kids would be getting a little box of candy, and they wouldn't get it if they weren't there.

"Every kid? Not just one for each family?" she asked. "Babies, too?"

I knew what she was thinking. Her baby sister Cacky was too little for candy herself, but the others could eat hers. "I think so," I replied.

Thelma was gripped by a hoarse coughing spell and covered her mouth with a bare, chapped hand. When she recovered, she spit on the grass and said that they'd probably be there. She started up the street then turned back. "Ruth," she said, "if you see my brothers or sisters, don't say anything about Santa Claus 'cause Ma says not to expect anything. That way they won't be disappointed."

"Okay," I said. She continued up the street and I finished the steps, unable to stop thinking of her red, raw-looking hands.

In the afternoon I reminded Jeanne to iron our robes for the children's choir performance. "They're done already," she informed me proudly and showed me the short white cotton capes and flowing red ties hanging in the laundry room. "No, you don't have to try it on, Ruth. You'll get it all wrinkled."

This was to be my first big performance with Dan Border's choir, and I was quite excited. The choir had achieved a certain fame in our area, so it was a definite honor to belong to it. Children were seldom chosen as young as second-graders, but Jeanne had been and now I had, too. We had been rehearsing since the beginning of October and had sung at school, where Mr. Border taught, but tonight was going to be special.

While I was setting the table for supper, I talked to Mother about something I had been thinking about. "Did Grandma send something for us with Uncle Will?"

She didn't answer right away. "Why?" she asked.

"Well, do you remember how I helped her wind all that yarn last summer from those old sweaters?" She nodded. "Well, I just wondered if she made anything from that yarn. She was joking with me and said not to be surprised if something wooly grabbed me around the neck." Mother laughed. "So I thought maybe she meant wooly mittens or a wooly scarf."

"Well," said Mother, "I'm surprised, Ruth. You never want to know what you're getting for Christmas beforehand."

When I told her my idea, she smiled and went to the hall closet and brought out a stuffed pillowcase. "Look inside," she told me. I sat down on the floor and opened it. It was full of children's knitted mittens, caps, and scarves, all sizes. There was also a note from

Grandma that read: "Mary, do you know anyone who could use these? Ruth helped me wind the yarn last summer, so you might let her have first choice."

"I think you and Grandma have the same idea, don't you?" asked Mother. "You can take them over tomorrow, okay?" I agreed and finished setting the table.

Jeanne and I ate quickly and left for the church, carefully carrying our robes on their wire hangers. It was cold, dark, and windy; the white capes flapped against our faces as we hurried the short distance to the main street, turned the corner, and ran the block to the church. Just beyond, the frozen river lay trapped beneath the bridge.

"'Frosty wind made moan,'" gasped Jeanne as we opened the door to the basement and rushed downstairs to the warmth. We laughed at the line she had quoted from one of our choir songs. Mr. Border heard us and nodded, smiling. We joined the others, about twenty or so, took off our coats and put on our robes. Older kids helped younger ones with the floppy red bows, and then we lined up for Mr. Border's approval. After everyone had passed his scrutiny, we settled into our serious warm-ups and vocalizing. We practiced taking the pitch and beginning each song. Some of us moved to different sections of the choir for different songs, sometimes singing high parts, sometimes low. We rehearsed moving easily and quietly, following his subtle hand cues.

"Remember," he reminded us, "keep your eyes on me at all times. Don't look out at the people. I can always tell when you do that." I knew that was true; he had scolded me once when my eyes had briefly wandered. I had been so crushed that it never happened again.

Finally, we were ready, more than ready, and filed, shivering, up the outer stairway and into the main part of the church. We sat off to the side and waited till the service was ready to start. From where we sat, we could see most of the rest of the sanctuary.

Despite the gloomy weather the church was full. I spotted our family sitting in the third row on the side: Daddy on the aisle, then Gwen, Mother, Bobby, John, and Uncle Will. Sister and Jimmy were living in Pretoria, a small mining town less than a mile away. We would be seeing them on Christmas Day. I was surprised that our dad was there, because Mother had said he was feeling really tired.

He was worried, she said, about the store and money and whether people were going to pay their bills.

I looked around and saw a lot of other people I knew. Sure enough, there was the Shaffer family, every single person from Mrs. Shaffer down to the baby. Seven in all. Six little boxes of candy.

Then the service started. A medley of familiar carols rose in wheezy breaths and filled our little church as Miss Watson pumped and played the old organ with energy and enthusiasm. Reverend Ormston greeted the congregation and led in the singing of "Oh, Little Town of Bethlehem" and "Away in a Manger." Next he read the scripture of the Christmas story. As I listened, I looked at the pine branches and candles that adorned the altar and window sills and thought how pretty everything was. I decided I would memorize these scriptures for next year.

As soon as the scripture was finished, the minister announced the children's choir and the songs we were going to sing. At the signal from Mr. Border we stood up and quietly took our places on the platform. He stood in front of us and seemed to be gathering us in with his eyes. At last, satisfied that we were ready, he raised the pitchpipe and blew the pitch. We hummed softly and then began to sing, the first phrase in a clear, pure unison, then breaking out into four-part treble harmony:

"In the bleak midwinter, frosty wind made moan,
Earth stood hard as iron, water like a stone;
Snow had fallen, snow on snow,
Snow on snow,
In the bleak midwinter, long ago."

I heard my dad clear his throat and wanted to look at him but didn't dare. There was scattered coughing from around the church, especially from the row where the Shaffers sat. We sang the last verse, which I liked especially because it sounded like a kid's thoughts, starting with "What can I give Him, poor as I am?"

People shifted a little then settled for the next song, "Lo, How a Rose E'er Blooming." When it was finished, Mr. Border seemed to relax a little, for a tiny smile appeared briefly and he nodded ever so slightly. Several of us shifted to different places, quickly, quietly, ready for "Jesu Bambino," and we began. I loved this song, the way it moved smoothly and gracefully down the scale in the first line, then back up again, the words and melody sounding so achingly simple and sweet. But, oh, when the descant was added, a boy's clear, high soprano, smooth and controlled, Harold Ringler at his best before his voice changed, my heart, or something, seemed to soar with the words "The angels sang, the shepherds sang, the whole wide world rejoiced."

Mr. Border had warned us of this: "Don't get carried away so that you sing louder or harder than we've practiced it because the beauty of the song makes you feel especially full. Just keep watching me and singing it the way I've taught you."

Then we sang "Angels We Have Heard on High" with its wonderful Gloria chorus, with the parts all seeming to move differently and yet coming back together just right with "in excelsis De-e-o!" Our last song was "O Holy Night." "Fall on your knees," we sang. "Oh, hear the angel voices! O night divine! O night when Christ was born!" I wanted so badly to look at my family, at other people, at my friends in the congregation, to see whether they realized that Something Mysterious was here, was happening, and that the music was bringing it close.

Then it was over, our part of the service was finished, and we walked back to our seats on the side. Jeanne had ended up beside me, and as we sat down, we looked at each other with great satisfaction.

Mr. Border had told us the minister was going to speak for about five minutes before the last carol. I thought I would probably just daydream through his talk until I heard him say, "This is the bleak midwinter of 1935." It took me by surprise. I thought somehow that phrase just referred to when Jesus was born, but he had definitely said *1935*. And then he said another strange thing, that the *bleakness* (I didn't know that *was* a word) was not only of gray weather, ice, and frosty wind, but also of the spirit, of the despair of the Depression, of the pain of unrelenting illness and of the grief at failure and loss, of the loneliness and heartbreak at death of loved ones, and of the sadness of children denied simple pleasures, opportunities, and even anticipation.

"This incomplete list of human conditions is not one that I found in a book," he said, "but is one compiled from real lives of members of our congregation, of people in our town, and in the larger community of towns surrounding us."

I sat up. I know people like that, I thought. Poor Mrs. Shaffer, whose husband died so young. Her kids, who are not supposed to expect anything wonderful to happen. Girly Brallier, who sits twisted up in a wheelchair and whose gurgling speech frightens children. My own father, who is worried sick about the store and money. Who is sitting with eyes glazed over with tears, trying not to blink.

"What does Christmas have to do with *our* bleak midwinter? How does Christmas transform our landscape?" I didn't understand these questions or some of the other stuff he said. How can Christmas change the Depression or bring back someone who died or heal someone who is sick? What I did understand was that when we do a kindness for people who are in need, it makes God happy, so it's like a gift to Him. And somehow, that makes us happy too, even though there are things in our world that are making us sad.

Reverend Ormston ended by reading the last verse of the "bleak midwinter" carol. Since it was one of our choir songs, we all knew it. Once he started it, I looked around and realized we were all saying it with him:

"What can I give Him, poor as I am?
If I were a shepherd, I would bring a lamb;
If I were a wiseman, I would do my part;
Yet what I can I give him: give my heart."

After we sang "Silent Night" and the minister gave the benediction, he reminded the children that there was a gift waiting for them. "Do you know what it is?" he asked, knowing very well that was the main reason for many of them to be there.

"Candy!" they shouted.

He laughed. "That's right, boys and girls! But I'm happy to tell you that there's another gift." There was a quick intake of breath from the children, and he went on. "When you come up to get your box of candy, you will also receive a beautiful—" he paused and leaned down to pick up something from behind the pulpit, "—ORANGE!" He held it up and the children applauded; some of them even squealed. "These were donated by our good friend, Jim Mugridge, from JIMANDAD'S store. In these hard times this is a very generous gift. Let's tell Mr. Mugridge thank you."

"Thank you, Mr. Mugridge!" the kids sang out. I was astonished. He had not mentioned a thing about oranges. Even in our family, oranges, though not rare, were a real treat. I looked over at my father; he nodded and smiled to acknowledge the children's thanks. Then he glanced at my mother as if to gauge her response. After a couple seconds she gave him a look, a sort of smile, and he seemed to relax, reassured.

All the children lined up and moved happily past the minister and the Sunday school superintendent, taking first from the table a little box of candy with its woven string handle and then an orange from the basket I had seen earlier at the store. We choir kids were the last to pick up our treats. While we waited patiently, Mr. Border told us he was quite pleased with our performance, and he wished us a Merry Christmas. Jeanne and I gave our robes to Mother to carry for us so that we could get our candy and oranges home without dropping them. The rest of the family went on ahead of us.

It was really dark by the time we got home, and it seemed so late, but it was just a little before eight o'clock. Gwen and I didn't know what to do with ourselves, so about 8:20 we decided to go to bed since that would make the morning come faster, or so we were told.

However, long after Gwen had gone to sleep, I was still relishing the details of my busy day. I heard talking and laughing from downstairs as the rest of the family decorated the tree. I wished that I could have been down there with them. Then I remembered the package under the bed and got out and down on my knees to retrieve it. I sat on the edge of the bed for a while and thought about something I had to do. Finally, I made up my mind. I felt around on Mother's dresser for the little tablet and pencil she always kept there and went into the bathroom, turning on the light. I sat down and figured out some stuff.

Then I went out to the top of the stairs. "Mother," I called out. The noise went on. I called louder.

Mother appeared at the bottom of the stairs. "Ruth," she said, "is there something wrong?"

I asked her whether she could come upstairs so I could ask her something. She came up right away, and we sat on the top step. I showed her the gifts in my bag and asked her what she thought about my new idea.

"It seems nice, but we'll have to ask Daddy. He is having a lot of trouble paying the store bills right now, and you know he spent a good bit on the oranges for the church."

"I know, but he won't have to spend anything more, I'm sure," I argued.

"Well, I'll ask him and see what he says." Mother started downstairs at the same time that Daddy appeared at the bottom.

"Is she all right?" he asked.

"Oh, Jim, there's nothing wrong with her. She's just worried about the Shaffers, that they're not having much of a Christmas."

"They're not, Daddy! They're not even supposed to *hope* for anything!" I went down several steps and decided to explain it all to him. "I have it all written down here, how we could get something for each one. I already have a coloring book and a box of crayons that Thelma would like." I decided not to give away my gifts for Gwen and Jeanne.

"But how could we get the others anything?" asked Mother. "It's too late."

"If John and Bob and Jeanne could go down to the store, if you'd let them have the key, they could use this list and get everything real fast. There's nothing that costs very much, no more than about twenty cents for each kid, except for that one thing that's for all of them." I was speaking really fast because I felt a small glimmer of optimism. I continued my plea. "I think maybe John would give us some money. Bob and Jeanne, too, if they have any. Can I ask them? Please, Daddy."

He looked at the list and then at me. "Go ahead if you want to."

I ran down the rest of the steps and into the playroom. I deliberately avoided looking at the Christmas tree and started to tell Jeanne, Bob, and John about going to the store. Then I stopped. "John, do you still have any money?"

"Why?" he asked. "I already gave you thirty cents. What are you doing down here now anyway?"

Mother came into the room and explained about the Shaffers. "She feels bad that her friends won't be getting any gifts."

"Actually," I interrupted, "they will be getting some mittens and other stuff that Grandma made. But nothing to play with." I paused, thinking of something. "I'll polish your shoes once a week for a month, John." I had been about to say for a year but caught myself in time. No need to put myself into slavery. However, John was feeling generous, and I didn't have to promise him anything else.

He pulled out a handful of change. "Will this be enough?" he asked.

I looked it over quickly. "Maybe. Almost. I think we need about fifty cents more." I glanced at Jeanne and Bob.

"I can put in fifteen cents," said Jeanne.

"Here's a quarter," offered Bob.

"Whatever you buy," our dad instructed, "be sure to write it down. Put the money and the receipt in an envelope on Romaine's desk where she can see it first thing Thursday morning. Here's the key."

"Don't be long," said Mother. "It's getting late."

They were back in less than half an hour, feeling very satisfied with themselves. Mother let me stay up long enough to check their purchases, after the others promised to wrap the gifts. But I was not finished.

"When will they get their presents?" I persisted.

"Well," said Mother, "I told Mrs. Shaffer I would send over a pot of chicken and noodles sometime around noon if she wanted them."

"What did she say?" I asked.

"She thanked me," Mother replied. "You could take the presents over then."

"No," I said, "I want them to have them when they get up in the morning."

Mother looked at me for a moment. At last she said, "Well, if you want to get up in the morning and take them over before they get up, that would be about seven o'clock."

"I can do it," I declared, since I knew I would be up early Christmas morning anyway. "I can take over the mittens and stuff at the same time."

"I'll help you," offered Jeanne. "We could sneak over and leave them in the kitchen, and they wouldn't even hear us."

"I could take some wood over, too, if it's okay," Bob suggested. "They probably can use it."

"It's okay, go ahead, Bob," said Dad, with a tired sigh. "They really need help. This isn't much, but it's all we can do."

"Now, Ruth, are you satisfied?" Mother asked with a smile. "We'll get everything wrapped; it'll be ready for you in the morning. You don't have to wake Daddy and me if the three of you can just run across the yard, leave the things, and come right back."

"Thank you, Mother, thank you, Daddy!" I gave each of them a hug and a kiss. I thanked Jeanne, Bob, and John, and started toward them, but they turned me around and headed me up the steps.

"This is way past your bedtime, young lady." John pretended to be stern and shook his finger at me.

I went upstairs and got back into bed, thinking about what a nice family I had, and before I knew it, it was morning. I tiptoed over in the dim light to look at the clock beside Mother and Daddy's bed. It was 6:50, so I got dressed in a hurry and went to wake Jeanne and Bob. Jeanne got out of bed right away and started to get dressed. Bob took longer to wake up, but all of a sudden he remembered what we were going to do.

We crept downstairs so we wouldn't wake anyone, put on our coats and caps, gathered up the bag of gifts, the pillowcase of knitted items, and the box of wood from the porch. The grass seemed icy so we went around by the sidewalk. Just as we were going up the steps, the kitchen light went on. We were so startled that we must have made some noise because Mrs. Shaffer came over to the door and peered out the window at us. At first she looked puzzled. Then she recognized us, smiled broadly, and opened the door.

"Are they up yet?" I whispered.

"No," she whispered back, "come in." We went in and stood awkwardly in the kitchen. "I was just getting the fire going."

Jeanne spoke up. "Mrs. Shaffer, we have some things for the kids. Where should we put them? Do you have a tree?"

She motioned us into the next room, dominated by a large table covered with oilcloth. A small branch from the pine tree in the front yard had been placed on the table in a quart Mason jar. It was decorated with a garland of linked rings of colored construction paper that Thelma had made in school. Six oranges and six tiny boxes of candy were arranged in a circle around the jar.

"That's very nice," said Jeanne. "Can we put the presents around the tree?" Mrs. Shaffer nodded.

We hurriedly emptied our bags and placed the wrapped gifts and the knitted things around the tree. It looked wonderful! We looked at each other happily and let out sighs of satisfaction. A sudden noise from upstairs sent us scurrying on tiptoe for the door and out onto the porch. Mrs. Shaffer closed the door quietly behind us, and we carefully made our way down the icy steps and ran across the grass for home.

Mother and Gwen were in the kitchen putting stuff on the table for breakfast. Mother always tried to enforce a rule about eating a good breakfast before opening any presents, but she usually relented if we ate at least a halfway decent one. So, before long, we stood at the door of the playroom, mesmerized at the sight of the lighted tree and the gifts underneath.

Gwen and I spotted our presents right away. The dolls that we had received the year before had new outfits: little sleeveless dresses with matching coats trimmed with bias tape. They were made from the same material as the playroom drapes, tan chintz with little bunches of white and pink flowers. My doll was seated in a small white rocking chair. Gwen's was lying on a little white bed with two men's handkerchiefs for sheets. We picked the dolls up immediately and started planning how we would trade the furniture back and forth as we played. I was delighted to find that I had a new box of crayons after all, and a new coloring book. And there was a gift for the two of us together, something we had wanted for some time, an Uncle Wiggly board game. We were so thrilled with our presents that we went to the kitchen to show them to Mother, as though she hadn't seen them before. And of course, we had our new mittens and warm, wooly caps and scarves, thanks to Grandma. What a wonderful Christmas!

That morning we put our dolls to bed, changed their clothes, sat them up in the rocking chair, colored in our coloring books, and talked Jeanne into playing Uncle Wiggly with us. I thought of the Shaffers and hoped they were having fun, too.

At noon, just before we sat down to our Christmas dinner, I heard Mother tell Bob "Be careful, it's hot," and saw that he was ready to carry a kettle of chicken and noodles over to our neighbors. Mother handed Jeanne a panful of waffles, covered them with a tea towel, and told her to tell Mrs. Shaffer to put them in the oven until they were ready for them. So, both our families had exactly the same meal, which I thought was nice.

After dinner when Daddy was snoozing in his chair and we girls were helping to clean up the kitchen, Mother looked out the window and exclaimed, "Oh, look who's here!" and there, coming up the sidewalk were five young Shaffers, resplendent in bright, colorful scarves, mittens, and caps that almost made you forget the worn old coats and jackets they were wearing. They came up the steps onto the porch, but before they had time to knock, I opened the door and called out, "Merry Christmas!"

They stood there grinning shyly, then spoke almost as one, "Merry Christmas!"

"Come in, come in!" my mother exclaimed warmly.

"Wipe your feet, everyone! Remember what Ma said," Thelma spoke firmly. Everyone wiped his or her feet thoroughly, even excessively, and stepped into the kitchen.

"Take off your stuff and come see our tree," I said and waited while they piled their wraps on the kitchen chairs. They followed me into the playroom and smiled and ah-ed in appreciation and then sat down on the floor to look at our presents.

"We got mittens, too," said Lorraine.

"And scarfs," added Danny.

"And caps, too," chimed in Beattie.

"I got that same coloring book," remarked Thelma. "It's nice."

"Yeah," I said, "I really like it. I got new colors, too. My old ones are all broken."

"Yeah, mine, too. I got new ones, too," said Thelma.

Gwen hadn't said much all along until now. "We got a doll bed and a rocking chair, so our dolls take turns."

"You didn't get new dolls, did you?" asked Beattie.

"No," I replied, "but our old dolls got new clothes."

"Yes'n they match the drapes in here," said Gwen. She hadn't mentioned it, so I didn't think she had noticed.

"I got a bag of marbles," whispered Emory, eager to join in.

"Were you surprised?" Jeanne asked.

Now they all wanted to talk at once: "We heard a noise...we came down...presents were all over the table... saw my name ...I saw the letter D...The mittens weren't wrapped, but they had my name...There was this little tiny package...I saw this big package and it had everybody's name on it...I laughed and laughed, I was so excited...Ma had tears...I saw my name!...We were all so happy!"

Jeanne, Gwen, Bob, and I sat there and laughed, it was so contagious. John came to the doorway and looked in. He pretended to be very puzzled and serious. "What's all this noise and excitement about? You'd think it was a holiday or something!"

All of us kids laughed and hollered louder than ever, "It is! It's Christmas!" John couldn't stay straight-faced after that. I think he realized then what his contribution had meant, and he had to smile.

Then Thelma spied our new game. "We got that, too! We got Uncle Wiggly, too!"

"We played it this morning," said Beattie. "Even our ma played it with us."

Just then Mother and Daddy came to the door to see what was happening. "Thelma," I whispered, "tell Mother what you told me about the dinner."

Thelma, usually shy around adults, didn't hesitate. "Oh, Mrs. Mugridge, your chicken and noodles were so good! We just ate and ate!"

"We did, too," said John.

"And the waffles were really good, too," said Beattie. "I ate two." I think she meant two quarters.

Then everyone had to tell how many waffles they had eaten, how many with just butter, how many with syrup. Of course, John beat everyone with four, and I don't mean quarters.

When all the waffle talk started, Daddy came in and sat down. I know he was still tired and worried about money and the store, but as he sat there and looked at the Shaffer kids and us, a kind of softness touched his face and made him seem younger somehow. This is what must have encouraged Danny to get up and go stand beside him.

"Mr. Mugridge," he started, "the oranges are real nice," and he paused. He looked at Thelma, who nodded back at him. "Thank you very much."

"You're welcome, Danny," my father said. "Did you eat yours yet?"

"No, you know wha-wha-what we're gonna do?" The little boy became so animated that he stammered.

"No, what, Danny?" asked Dad. I think it must have tickled him that his gift of oranges was the subject of discussions and planning.

"Our ma is gonna peel one orange every day, and then—" he interrupted himself. "Mr. Mugridge, do you know how many pieces there are in an orange?"

"I think at least eight," said my dad. "Maybe more."

"Yes, eight!" exclaimed Danny.

"And with our ma we have seven people," said Thelma, "so everybody gets one piece with one left over."

"So who gets the extra one?" asked Gwen.

"Today was the first day we did that, and we gave it to the baby," explained Thelma. "We'll decide each day, I guess."

"That way we each have a bit of orange every day instead of eating them all at once!" declared Beattie.

"Yeah," her brothers and sisters chorused.

"Well, I'm glad you like the oranges, kids," my father said. "I looked around the store and wondered what I could give the children at church on Christmas Eve that would be special, and that's what I came up with."

All at once I thought of the line from the "bleak midwinter" carol: *What can I give him, poor as I am?*

"Mr. Mugridge," said Danny, "did you know…that was the first orange I ever tasted!"

If I were a grocer…

The general store my father (Jim) co-owned with "Dad" (Fred) Bailey (circa 1930)

8

That Tuesday

That Tuesday, when Jeanne and I got to school, all wet and dripping, there were only about thirty kids present out of the eight grades, and by 10:30 we were the only ones left. Although no other part of Hollsopple except ours, below the railroad tracks, was likely to be flooded, all the other children had either been kept home or picked up. We had the entire three-room schoolhouse to ourselves, along with Miss Miller, my teacher, who had volunteered to stay until the last child had gone. She showed us the note that our dad had sent with someone else's father, asking that we be kept at school until someone came to get us, maybe by three but no later than four o'clock.

"I wonder why so late," I commented to Jeanne, who simply shrugged.

Miss Miller knew the answer to that. "Billy's dad said your father was busy moving things in the store up higher. Someone has borrowed the store pickup truck to move people to higher ground, and it should be back by the middle of the afternoon." She must have thought that our expressions were glum. "Don't worry, girls," she said. "You won't be bored. There are a lot of things you can do here if you want to."

"Like what?" I asked.

"Well," she replied, stalling a little, I thought, "you could wash the desks."

I looked at Jeanne. Was this supposed to be fun? To my surprise, Jeanne smiled and answered, "All right, we'll do it, won't we, Ruth?"

"I guess so," I mumbled and was surprised to hear Miss Miller laugh.

"We'll make it a contest," she said, getting up from her desk and the papers she had been correcting. "Let's go get some buckets of water first, and then I'll tell you how we'll do it."

We had to go down to the basement where there were cleaning supplies and a sink. It was the first time I had noticed anything but the boys' and girls' restrooms down there. (In fact, in class when we raised our hands to go to the restroom, we always said, "May I go to the basement?" For years afterward, the word *basement* evoked sights and smells of the musty, dark, damp school lavatory of my grade school years.) We ran water into four buckets and put soap stuff into two of them. We found cloths hanging over the pipes to use as cleaning rags, and then the three of us lugged everything upstairs to Miss Miller's room.

"Now," explained my teacher, "this is where the contest comes in. I'll start at the third-grade side, you two start at the first-grade side, and we'll meet in the middle. One of you will use the soapy water, and the other the clear water. Go over the whole desk but go as fast as you can. I'll bet I can beat you."

"Oh, no, you can't," laughed Jeanne, and I echoed her. We took the buckets to our respective sides and after a "Ready, set, go!" from Miss Miller, the contest began. Jeanne took the soapy bucket and started on the folding seat of the first desk and continued with the desk top and seat. I glanced over at Miss Miller. She was already about halfway down the row, she was working so fast! "Get going, Ruth! Don't waste time!" Jeanne whispered loudly. I wrung out the rag in the clear water and began wiping the desk she had washed; I couldn't help looking over at Miss Miller as I worked. She had finished washing the first row and now was using the clear water. She smiled at me and waved her rag a little, then went right back to work.

"Ruth! Hurry!" pleaded Jeanne, finishing the little desks in the first row. I really got busy then, making the cloth and the clear water fly, and hardly gave my teacher another glance as we raced down the rest of the first-graders' section and went on to the second-graders' three rows, with my desk in the middle of the second row. We scrubbed and splashed away until suddenly, there was Miss Miller, facing us.

"We're done!" she exclaimed. "I've finished twenty-two desks. How many have you done?"

We looked across the room and counted: twelve first-grade desks and eight second-grade ones. "Twenty," replied Jeanne, disappointed. "There were two of us and you still beat us."

"Don't feel bad," Miss Miller said. "I've had a lot of practice." We took the buckets back down to the basement, emptied them down the drain in the floor, and hung the cloths over the pipes. It was then when we started back upstairs that I thought of the flood; we had been so engrossed in the desk-scrubbing contest that I had forgotten the flood for the time being.

Back in my room I looked up at the large wall clock: 11:10. I wondered what was going on down in our end of town. I couldn't picture what a flood would look like. Would our house be covered with water? What were Mother and Gwen and Uncle Will doing? Mother had been ironing clothes that morning when we left, and Uncle Will and Gwen were still eating breakfast. Would firemen be riding around the streets in boats, stopping at upstairs windows to save people?

"Miss Miller," I ventured, "can Jeanne and I go outside down the hill a ways and see what's happening?"

"No, I'm sorry, Ruth," she answered, "you have to stay inside with me, since I'm responsible for you."

Jeanne thought of something. "Miss Miller," she asked, "is it okay for us to go upstairs to my room? We might be able to see something from the windows up there."

"Oh, yes, certainly," Miss Miller replied. "Come back and tell me what you can see."

We ran out of the room and upstairs. The sole of my left shoe was loose and flapping and sounded really loud when I ran, but I couldn't help it. I had tried to leave my boots on when I got to school, but Miss Miller had noticed and told me to take them off. I knew the school didn't like children to keep their boots on because their feet got too warm and smelly. I needed to take my shoe to the shoemaker, Mr. Ruis, but at the moment I didn't have a second pair to wear while it was being repaired. There weren't any shoes my size at our store, and no one had the time to take me to Bruno's, a little store beside the post office that sold all kinds of things, like bread and milk, pins and needles, soap and shoes.

Jeanne and I headed for the tall windows in the back of the room that held the fourth, fifth, and sixth grades. We had hoped to see our end of town, but the houses on the other side of the playground blocked our view. Disappointed, I turned away, but Jeanne pulled me back. "Ruth, look! Over there, at the river!" Away off to the right, past the railroad trestle, we could see the brown, swollen river, deeper and wider than I had ever seen it, surging and swirling on its way to Johnstown.

"Jeanne, look! There's someone's outhouse!" I pointed out to my sister, who nodded silently, awestruck. "I'm going to tell Miss Miller!" I flapped noisily out of the room, down the stairs and into the primary classroom, where I told my teacher what I had seen.

She shook her head sadly. "Someone told me this morning that the Stoneycreek[1] would be rising to a total of about fourteen feet today if the rain kept up. Things don't look too good for your end of town."

"Miss Miller," I ventured, "if you went with us, could we go out on the road and try to see down the hill?"

"Yes, of course," she replied, getting up from her desk and heading for the cloak room. "Tell Jeanne to get her coat and come down. We'll go out right now while there's a break in the rain."

I grabbed my coat and boots from the cloak room and ran up a couple of steps and called Jeanne. In a few minutes we were standing out on the hill road that went straight down into town, over the railroad tracks, past the movie theater, back our street, and on to the river.

"There's water all over our street!" exclaimed Jeanne. "I can't see the sidewalks at all!"

I stared, not believing my eyes. "The river is coming up the road!" I gasped. "How far can it come?"

"Don't worry," Miss Miller assured us. "It can't come over the railroad tracks." I must not have looked convinced. "Really, Ruth, you're safe up here. Come on, let's go in and eat our lunches." We started toward the school building. "Guess what I brought today— mashed potato candy!"

Jeanne and I exclaimed at the same time, "Our mother makes that!" and burst out laughing. We were still discussing the details of adding powdered sugar, creating different flavors, or making peanut butter roll-ups as we entered the building and went up the steps to my classroom.

We sat at Miss Miller's work table and opened our paper lunch bags. Jeanne and I had sandwiches of homemade bread and chopped-up beef from last night's roast mixed with mayonnaise and pickle relish to make the meat go further. We each had an apple to finish off our lunch.

I couldn't wait to see what Miss Miller had in her bag, but I didn't like to stare. I had noticed on other days that she really brought a lot of stuff. She must always have thought in the morning that she was going to be hungry, and then at lunchtime changed her mind. She usually had extra sandwiches that she couldn't eat because she said she was too full. Of course, there were children who were glad to do her the favor of taking them off her hands, kids who said that their mothers had forgotten to pack their lunches or that they had lost them on the way to school. Today I saw she had two peanut butter and jelly sandwiches, a cheese sandwich, a plain slice of buttered bread, and four hard-boiled eggs. In addition, she had three apples and about ten pieces of the mashed potato candy. We ended up trading sandwiches and helped her get rid of two of the eggs, plus some of the candy, which she happened to make just like Mother did, like a little jelly roll.

While we were eating, we talked a lot, sometimes about the food, sometimes about other things, like the children's choir that Jeanne and I were both in. In fact, it was because of Miss Miller that I was able to be in the choir as a second-grader. One afternoon in the previous September when all of our work was done, Miss Miller had happened to ask whether anyone wanted to do anything for the class, such as say a poem, tell a joke or riddle, or sing a song. I had an idea of what I wanted to do, but I wanted to wait till the end. Finally, after several riddles I raised my hand and told Miss Miller that I wanted to sing a song. I went up to the front and announced that I was going to sing "The Isle of Capri," a popular song that my sister Elizabeth liked to play on the piano. Even though Sister was married and living a mile away with Jimmy in Pretoria, she still liked to come home and play for everyone to sing.

I started singing and things seemed to be going okay until I noticed that the rest of the kids were all smiling and looking past me toward the doorway. I turned around and saw Mr. Border standing there listening to me, his finger to his lips, signaling to the children not to give him away. They all laughed to see my surprise but quieted down when he told me to finish. He stood there until the song was over, and he motioned me to the door. I went over to see what he wanted and was thrilled to hear him say, "Ruth, if you want to be in the children's chorus, ask your parents and come to practice with Jeanne next week, okay?" I nodded happily and watched him cross the hall to his classroom. I couldn't wait to tell Jeanne that I was going to be in Mr. Border's choir, too.

Now Miss Miller often asked me about the choir, how I liked being in it, and what songs we were working on, so it didn't surprise me when she started talking about it again.

"Girls, I'd like to go out and look down the street again if you don't mind, just to see how high the water is, but then when we come back in, I was wondering whether you would sing one of your chorus songs for me?" Of course, we were agreeable on both counts. We donned our coats and boots for the second time and tramped out onto the road to check on the flood.

We gazed in silence at the river encroaching on our town below, brown water lapping at porch steps and telephone poles, swirling around bristly winter hedges, and reaching up as though to choke the SLOW road sign at the big curve.

Finally, Jeanne spoke. "You can hardly see where the street is anymore."

"I know," I wondered out loud. "How will the cars know where to drive?"

"They probably won't be driving down that street," said Miss Miller. "I think maybe their engines would stop."

Jeanne and I looked at each other with the same question: Are Mother and Gwen and Uncle Will still at home?

Before we put our worried thought into words, Miss Miller took us each by the hand and started back to the school building. "I'm sure your family is all right, girls." She sounded very confident. "They've had a lot of time to get everyone from your end of town to other places. I know they'll be coming for you as soon as they can." She began to run, pulling us along. "Let's hurry! It's starting to rain again."

More rain! How many days had it been now, four or five? I think people had been stopping to talk to our dad every evening for a long time, reporting on the river and how many feet it had risen in the last day. I only knew that he had been spending long evenings at the store, trying to move bulk stuff that would be spoiled in case of a flood, like rice and beans. I knew he was really worried, because the store, just a short block from our house, was pretty close to the river.

We stomped back into the school, trying to shake off as much water as we could. It was really odd, laughing and talking and stamping our feet on the stairs up to my room, and at the same time, being the only people in the whole building. I stopped at the top of the steps to savor the strangeness of the whole day. Jeanne turned back to look at me; I think she was feeling the same thing, but we couldn't seem to put it into words, so we just left our wraps in the cloakroom and joined Miss Miller.

"I'm ready to hear a song," she announced as she sat down at her desk, and we were ready to sing one, having already decided on "The Ash Grove," a family favorite because it's a Welsh folk melody with nice harmony. We stood at the front of the room, facing our teacher, and sang the gentle, poignant song of memories and homesickness. I loved the song, because it made me think of Morgan's Grove, up above the railroad tracks, but it's hard for me now to understand this choice for children, it's so sad. (Or is it just sad to me now?)

"The ash grove, how graceful, how plainly 'tis speaking,
   The wind through it playing has language for me.
   Whenever the light through its branches is breaking
   A host of kind faces is gazing on me.
   The friends of my childhood again are before me,
   Each step wakes a memory as freely I roam.
   With soft whispers laden its leaves rustle o'er me,
   The ash grove, the ash grove alone is my home."

We had been taught to sing it in a very simple, unemotional way, so I was always amazed to see people reacting with tears, as Miss Miller was.

"That's really pretty, girls," she said, dabbing at her eyes with a hanky. "You sound nice together."

"Thank you," Jeanne replied, "but you should hear the way the chorus sounds with four-part harmony."

"And a descant," I put in, pleased to know this distinction. "Harold Ringler sings a descant." When she didn't say anything, I added, "That's a high part that's different from the rest."

"That's right," she nodded. "Harold still has a high voice. I heard the chorus sing at the Christmas service. It was beautiful…your first concert, right?" I had forgotten that she had taught most of the members of the chorus. "Would you like to sing anything else for me?"

We sang a couple of other songs for her and then went upstairs to see the flood from that angle again. We could see how strong the current was as the river surged and raced toward Johnstown, tree branches, outhouses, and porches caught up in a kind of unwilling excitement and pressing, swelling, racing to an unknown destination.

I heard Jeanne gasp. "What?" I asked sharply.

"Nothing, nothing," she said hastily. "I thought I saw something, but I was wrong."

We watched a little longer before going downstairs to tell Miss Miller what we had seen. As we talked, I looked up at the clock. Only 1:30. I sighed heavily, wondering what was happening to the rest of our family, to our house, and the store.

"It's hard waiting like this, isn't it?" said Miss Miller, noticing my glance at the clock. I nodded despondently and went to sit down at my desk in the middle of the second-grade rows. Jeanne had found a book to read and seemed occupied for the time being. I pulled out my spelling book and looked at the current assignment. I copied the words a couple of times each and put the book away. I had done all my arithmetic problems the day before, so there was no point in just looking at them now.

I cleaned out my desk and threw away all the papers I had drawn pictures on, thinking for the hundredth time how lucky we were that Pennsylvania gave every child a new tablet and pencil once a month. I noted that I had two loose tablet backs and decided to take them home for the next time I had a hole in my shoe. Grandma had shown me how to draw on the cardboard around the front of my shoe and then trim it to fit inside. The pressed cardboard, thin and flexible, was perfect for this task and usually provided a couple of additional days of shoewear. I rearranged my books and sharpened my one good pencil. Finally, I put my head down on my desk, thinking that maybe I could go to sleep for a few minutes. After what seemed like a long time of thinking and not sleeping, I looked up at the clock again. Ten till two. Where was everyone? Why didn't they come for us?

I jiggled my foot, flapping the loose sole. I tried different rhythms: *flap, flappity flap, flap flap...*

"Ruth." Both Jeanne and Miss Miller had spoken at the same time. Jeanne was shaking her head and frowning at me, but Miss Miller was smiling and motioning me to her desk. "I'm going to make some copies of pictures for the classes. Would you like to help me?"

Now that sounded interesting. Every month each class would get pictures with seasonal or holiday themes to color. For instance, this month, March, first-graders colored pictures of children flying kites; second-graders, windmills and fields of tulips; third-graders, mother and baby animals. All of these pictures had been colored and then mounted above the blackboards. I had wondered how Miss Miller made these copies, and now I would find out.

We went over to her work table, where I saw what looked like a pan of grape Jell-o. She explained that this was a hectograph and showed me what she called master copies of the April pictures: Easter baskets, rabbits, wildflowers, and children in raincoats walking in the rain with umbrellas. She picked up the master copy of the Easter basket and started to place it carefully on the Jell-o stuff, beginning at one end. She pressed out wrinkles as she went until the whole page was lying flat. She rubbed her hand over it a couple of times, and then she picked up one end and peeled the paper off again. Somehow the design was transferred to the dark purple below.

"Now we're ready to make copies," she announced. At this, Jeanne came over to see what was going on. Miss Miller showed us how to put the blank sheets on one at a time, smooth them out, and pull them up...transformed! I was delighted with the process and couldn't wait to get started. Even spoiling two sheets of paper didn't discourage me, since Miss Miller was very patient and sympathetic. "That happens to me sometimes, too," she confided. "Just try again and don't worry if there's a little wrinkle. We can still use it." Finally, on the third try I got the hang of it and produced a nearly perfect design.

"Now, Jeanne," my teacher announced, "I have two hectographs. Would you like to work on the other one?" Of course, the answer was yes. Jeanne picked the rabbit design and let Miss Miller start it for her by laying the master copy on the gelatin bed, as she called it. She soon caught up with me and in no time, well, maybe forty-five minutes, we had all of the April pictures completed. We even thought that if we had a break and a snack (maybe Miss Miller's leftover lunch?), we could attempt the May designs, but she laughed and said no, that she needed to clean up everything before it got late. We helped her straighten things up a little, then went upstairs to look out the windows.

Again we were appalled at the tumbling debris we caught sight of in the rushing waters. "I'm sure glad we put our sleds in the playhouse," I told Jeanne, "or they'd probably be gone now, too."

Jeanne just kept looking out the window and didn't say anything. Then I saw something else. "Jeanne, look over there at the railroad trestle. I just saw some people walking off this end of it. Oh," I said, disappointed, "you can't see them now. They're behind the trees."

Now Jeanne looked at me. "You know what that probably means."

"No, what?"

"I bet that the regular bridge is out," she answered.

"You mean washed away?" I couldn't imagine such a thing.

"Something like that," she said. We continued watching in silence, overwhelmed by the destructive force of our river.

Finally, we went downstairs to my room and looked up at the clock: 3:15. Surely they would be coming soon. Daddy's note had said maybe by three o'clock.

I felt a funny kind of trembling in my chest and put my head down on my arms to try to stop it. I didn't want to cry. I never cried when I was hurt or upset. I remember always feeling this way, but especially so since our brother Bob had broken his arm a year or so before, and hadn't cried at all, even though no anesthetic was used in setting it. The doctor had told him he was very brave. However, Bob didn't brag about it, since he had been sledriding without permission and was a little embarrassed about the whole thing. I was impressed, though, and wanted to be brave like him. The only things that made me cry were sad books or movies.

"Ruth! Ruth!" Jeanne was shaking me and saying my name really loudly. I must have fallen asleep because I couldn't remember where I was for a moment. I looked around the schoolroom.

"Why's it so dark?" I wondered.

"The electricity's gone off all over town," she replied, "but, Ruth, listen! Daddy's outside in the truck. He's come for us!"

"Where's Miss Miller?" I asked her, starting to the cloakroom for my boots and coat.

"She's outside talking to him," said Jeanne, slipping into her coat. "We were both asleep, and she heard the truck coming up the hill."

We had our coats and boots on and were all ready to leave when Miss Miller came up the stairs, carrying a grocery bag. She noticed me looking at it and smiled. "A gift from your father. Things from the store that would spoil with the electricity off, but that I can definitely make use of."

For some reason I hadn't thought of Miss Miller cooking meals, cutting up vegetables, making soup and other stuff. I always pictured her at home grading papers and reading books, so this was a new idea for me.

Miss Miller went on. "Your father says it'll probably take a couple of weeks to clean up the parts of town that are flooded, so we won't have school for a while. You may want to take home all your books."

I hadn't thought about that at all. I thought that the water would simply go down, and in a couple days everything would go back to the way it had been. Jeanne went upstairs for her books, and I got mine from my desk. On my way out of the room I stopped at my teacher's desk and thanked her for staying with us all day. "We had fun," I told her and really meant it.

Jeanne looked in the door and said, "Thank you very much, Miss Miller. I'd like to help you with the hectograph sometime again if you'd let me."

"Oh, I would, too," I chimed in, wishing that I had thought of it first.

"Thank you, girls, for helping me with everything," Miss Miller spoke as she gathered up her purse, her case with school materials, and the bag of groceries. She flipped the light switch even though there was no power. "I don't want the light on in my room after the electricity comes back on." We went down the steps with her and out the door and waited while she locked it. We walked over to the side street where her car was parked in front of the store truck and said goodbye to her again. Then we ran over to the truck, opened the door, threw our things inside, and jumped up on the seat beside Daddy. He put his arms around us, and we hugged and kissed him as though it had been days since we had seen him instead of just that morning.

We kept talking and asking him questions about where everyone was and how high the water was and whether the store was okay. He finally was able to get a word in to let us know that everyone was safe, that the river was still rising, and that there was water in the store.

"Where're Mother and Denny?" I wanted to know. "And Uncle Will?"

"They're up at Sister and Jimmy's. That's where we're going," he answered as he turned the truck around and started down the hill. He paused before turning left on the way to Pretoria. It was getting dark, and the only lights were those of the truck, hitting and skipping over bumps and little hills in the road, shining over the railroad tracks and down over the restless, dark water like two paths of golden light reaching back to our end of town.

"It's funny, but it almost looks pretty," Jeanne murmured.

"Until you see it in the daytime," was our dad's reply. "So much has been destroyed or washed away. I'll tell you more about it tonight." His face looked so tired, his voice was kind of shaky, and he cleared his throat the way he often did when something upset or touched him.

I wanted to tell him everything we had done at school that day, cleaning the desks, helping with the hectograph pictures, and watching the path of the Stoneycreek from the upstairs window, but when I started to say something, Jeanne squeezed my hand several times so hard that I realized she wanted me to be quiet. So no one said anything more as the truck turned and chugged up the darkened hillside road, past houses with windows lit by candles and kerosene lamps. I couldn't wait to see the rest of our family. I'll have plenty of time, I told myself, to tell everyone about our exciting day.

And so we came to Pretoria, where we spent the first night of the flood.

Those brothers of mine, Bob and John (circa *1930*) *Love the kneesocks!*

9

AFTERFLOOD

Pretoria was a small coal mining town built on the side of a hill, about a mile from Hollsopple. It had mostly company houses and a large boarding house, where our sister Elizabeth and her husband Jimmy lived in a small apartment. Daddy parked the truck in front of the boarding house, and Jeanne and I made several trips, helping him carry the bags and bags of groceries up to the second floor, where the rest of the family was waiting. This is interesting, I thought. Where is everyone going to sleep?

Gwen must have been listening for us because, before we had reached the top on the second trip, she opened the door and called down to us. "Jeanne! Ruth! I was in the flood! I rode in a boat! Mother has clothes for us in a suitcase!" For some reason Gwen and I were really intrigued with having our clothes packed in a suitcase, taking them out and putting them on. We didn't very often go anywhere that we stayed overnight, but when we did, a large part of the pleasure came from taking our clothes from a suitcase.

"Where's Bob?" asked Jeanne, and at that moment he walked out of the bedroom, all neat and clean as though he had just changed clothes. He carried an armful of dirty clothes that he held out to Mother.

"Where are you going?" I asked him. "Why'd you change clothes?"

"My pants got all wet," he answered.

"Why?" I persisted. "How'd you get home?" Bob was a ninth-grader at Cochran Jr. High in Johnstown, while John was a senior at Johnstown Central. I knew Bob had ridden to school that morning with John and some of his friends, but what happened after that?

Daddy answered for him. "John came home early to help at the store, and he left a message for Bob to catch a ride home, so he did."

"Do you know what I did all day?" Bob asked and continued

without waiting for an answer. "I ran all over the school taking messages to kids whose parents had come to pick them up. Then I'd go back to the office and they'd send me off for someone else. Finally, when school let out, I got a ride with a bunch of kids who said they'd take me home. But they left me off on the other side of the river 'cause the bridge is out, so I walked over on the railroad bridge."

He looked sideways at Mother and Daddy. People weren't supposed to play or walk on the trestle, but a lot of the kids Bob's age did it all the time. He had told me before that it wasn't really dangerous, that all that could happen was that if you fell between the ties, you'd just go into the water below. When I'd asked him what would happen if a train came, he said you'd usually have time to get out of the way. Besides, most people were familiar with the trains' coming and going and wouldn't walk across at those times.

Before I could ask another question, Bob continued. "Some firemen saw me coming down off the tracks on my way to the store. They told me the current was too strong and that I should just wait at one of the houses above the tracks. There was water everywhere. So I waited at Knapps' and in a little while the firemen brought Mother and Denny and Uncle Will to the railroad tracks—"

"In a boat!" hollered Gwen. "Everybody on our street kept leaving, and we kept staying and staying and staying, and then the firemen came in a boat and said we had to leave, so Mother said okay, and that's when we left." She paused to take a breath, and Mother pulled her over to sit on her lap in the rocker.

"You've had a busy day, Denny. What would you think of a little nap before we eat supper?" Mother stroked Gwen's black curly hair as she spoke.

"I want to tell them about the flood," Gwen complained. "They weren't in it like we were." I felt a wave of irrational envy that Gwen had experienced the flood more directly than Jeanne and I had. Now it seemed that our whole day had been spent in irrelevant activity, while hers was really involved. She was actually in a boat in the flood waters! It made me really grumpy.

"You can tell them about it while we eat," Mother murmured quietly as she rocked. "And you can tell them how you helped me pack the suitcase with clothes for everyone."

Gwen was getting drowsy. "Underwear for everyone…socks for everyone…shirts for everyone…"

"Daddy...Uncle Will...John..." Mother continued softly. "Bob...Jeanne...Ruth...you..."

"Uh huh," Gwen sighed sleepily, and her eyes closed.

"Mother," I asked quietly so that I wouldn't waken Gwen, "where did the Shaffers go?"

"I'm not sure," she whispered, "but I saw them leave about 11 o'clock. They probably went up on the ridge to their grandpa's." That settled a question that had worried me all day.

Daddy was helping to put the groceries away. "Jeanne and Ruth, do you want to help Sister get supper on the table? I think every-body's hungry."

"What are we having?" I asked as I went to the cupboard for dishes.

"Daddy sent meat from the store, and Mother sent a lot of canned vegetables from the cellar before the water got too high, so we're having soup," replied Sister. "And Mother sent all the bread in the house, so I made a big bread pudding. And Dad," she went on, "that was really smart thinking on your part to have someone gather up the wood and coal before it got too wet. We can definitely use it here if everybody is staying for a while."

"No matter how long," added Jimmy. "You're welcome to stay as long as you need to. You've sure helped us a lot."

The soup smelled wonderful, I thought, as we carefully carried the steaming bowls to the table. I returned to the counter by the stove for the bread pudding, still warm and sweet from the oven. Thoughts of the food we were about to eat made me think of the store; I won-dered whether there would be a lot of stuff spoiled and asked Daddy about it.

"Some people came in and bought things on their way out of town, so that helped," he said. "We knew the electricity would prob-ably be going off, and there wouldn't be any refrigeration available."

"So what'd you do?" asked Bob.

"We called the Red Cross pretty early and told them we had food to donate for flood victims here in town if they could pick it up, so they did. Mr. Bailey sent some things back to his wife that they could use, too," Dad explained. My grouchiness returned as I felt a wave of resentment toward his partner, Fred Bailey, whom everyone called Dad, who lived in a higher part of town unaffected by the flood. "By the way," he went on, "John and Uncle Will are staying at the Baileys' until the flood waters go down and the town gets cleaned up."

"Are their clothes in our suitcase?" I wondered out loud. Why is that so funny, I thought, when the others all laughed.

"No," Daddy smiled, "your mother packed a separate one for them. We'll see them during the day and for most meals."

We were sitting at the table by this time, except for Mother and Denny, who were still in the rocking chair. At the sound of the laughing Gwen stirred and woke up from her brief nap. She climbed off Mother's lap and came over to the table. "I remember now what I wanted to tell you," she said and paused to yawn widely. Jeanne and I waited patiently through that yawn and then a second one before our little sister could speak. When the news came, I was dumbstruck. "The playhouse is gone!" she announced. "The flood took the playhouse!"

I looked from her to Mother and Dad, thinking surely they would scold her for teasing me, but they didn't. Their solemn faces told me the truth.

"And not just the playhouse," Denny went on. "The garage is gone, the chicken coop is gone, and the back steps are gone." She paused a few seconds. "Yes, and the side steps are gone."

For the first time that day I felt such a heavy weight of loss and sadness that I couldn't speak. I turned to Jeanne and was surprised by her expression, not one of shock but of sympathy. "Did you know about it?" I demanded suspiciously.

"I thought I saw it when we were upstairs at school," she admitted, "you know, down where you could see the river going out of town. I saw a bunch of things, like outhouses and garages, so I wasn't real sure. I didn't want to make you feel bad when I wasn't sure." She looked so miserable I couldn't be mad at her.

"Daddy," asked Gwen very seriously, "what will people do now without outhouses?" Bob snickered, and Daddy frowned at him.

"As soon as the water goes down and the town gets cleaned up," he replied, "probably the WPA or the CCC will come in and set up new ones. It'll be taken care of, don't worry. That'll be one of the first things the government will do. I don't think people will be allowed back in their houses until that's done."

"Just the same," Gwen added, "I'm glad our bathroom is inside, and we don't have to wait for a new outhouse." We thought she was finished, but she thought of something else. "But, Daddy, an out-house is nice to have when you're playing outside and don't have time to go inside to the bathroom." She seemed pleased when every-body laughed, so she added, "So maybe we could get one."

I couldn't see why that was so funny or how people could be laughing when the playhouse, our wonderful playhouse, was gone. All the kids in the neighborhood gathered there to play. I was unable to suppress a funny gulp, a sob, really, at the thought of all our sleds simply...gone. Our playhouse, gone.

Everybody turned to look at me, and I ground my teeth together to keep from crying. I was glad when Gwen asked another silly question.

"Daddy, the water came up in the store, didn't it?"

He nodded, his mouth full of bread pudding.

She continued. "Did you move everything so stuff wouldn't get wet?"

"Everything that we could," he managed to reply.

"Did you move the counter right inside the door?" she persisted.

"What did it have in it?" he asked. I couldn't believe that Daddy would be teasing her at such a serious time as this. He knew what the counter had in it.

"You know, Daddy," she said, "penny candy!"

He pushed his chair back from the table and went over to the bags of groceries we had carried in and placed on the floor. He looked in several bags before thrusting his hand in one and pulling it out, full of candy. He came back to the table and emptied his hand with a flourish. "You mean this stuff?" Everybody laughed at Gwen's happy gasp and her delighted expression.

"Did you bring it all home?" she exclaimed, incredulous at such a possibility.

"No," he replied, "Mr. Bailey and I divided what was loose in the display case since we wouldn't be able to sell it after the flood. We just dumped it in two bags to bring home. The rest of the candy in boxes was stored on the second floor with other things. So, are any of your favorites there?"

"Sure, all of these, gumdrops, suckers, licorish, everything!" She reached out to gather up the candy. I couldn't believe it. Did she think all that candy was for her? Fortunately, Mother straightened things out and told Denny that the candy was for everyone, not just her. That was all right with her. She had such a sunny nature that things didn't make her mad at all. Not like me; I sometimes felt really grouchy inside. But Gwen just took a piece of candy around to everyone, enjoying her own generosity. She then went over to the grocery bag full of candy on the floor.

"My goodness," she marveled, "we'll never run out of candy!" She was about to rummage both hands down inside the bag when Mother stopped her and put the candy in a cupboard.

"You can give everybody a piece tomorrow after dinner, Gwen," Mother told her. "That way it'll last a long time."

"We have so much, maybe I'll give them two," Gwen said, testing Mother's reaction.

"We'll see," was her non-committal response.

I was becoming impatient with all this talk of outhouses and candy when the really important matter was our playhouse being gone. "Did you see it happen?" I asked Mother. "Our playhouse…" I couldn't even think of the words to express the tragedy: washed away, swept away, destroyed, smashed? "Was it all broken up?" I couldn't imagine the backyard without it, it was so painful.

"It was floating," Gwen answered before Mother had a chance. "Uncle Will and I saw it floating, and we told Mother."

Mother nodded. "Everything else seemed to be breaking up, the outhouses, chicken coops, garages, everything but the playhouse. I think it was made so well, so tight, that it just floated away."

"Kind of bouncing-like and turning sideways," added Gwen. "At first I thought it was going up into Bensons' yard, but it didn't."

I pictured the neat little house: Oh, the shingled roof, the little windows that went up and down, the light you could turn off and on, the door knob, the door that latched…our wonderful playhouse, drenched and buffeted and pounded by the dirty brown flood waters, pulled this way and that by the swirling, surging waves that washed over our end of town from three sides, and it just…floated away.

Years later, when people asked me how we could have had such a well-built, obviously expensive playhouse in the midst of the Depression, I explained what I knew about the situation. In the early thirties several out-of-work carpenters had approached our dad and Mr. Bailey about the large amount of money the men owed to JIMANDAD'S, one of the Regal stores. Their idea was to build something that the store or our two families could use, a garage, maybe an addition to a house, whatever was needed, as long as the debt was paid. What the two partners came up with was two playhouses, since there were children in each family. Daddy and Mr. Bailey provided the materials and plans, and the carpenters, the work. Perhaps they thought that in an emergency someone could live in the playhouses, I don't know.

Anyway, even though the store would have been better off if the debt had been repaid with money, we children loved the bartered playhouse. Padded with scraps and remnants of old blankets and sheets, our five sleds became sofas and beds, even hospital beds after our tonsillectomies. Wooden orange crates played counters, cupboards, and benches, whatever we needed them to be. Scrubbing the floor, washing windows, shaking the worn rag rugs, greeting the Fuller Brush salesman gave us a certain sense of housewifely pride and industry, as did cooking a tomato in a little tin saucepan on Jeanne's miniature electric stove.

I sat in empty despair at the table, wondering what life would be like without the playhouse. I didn't pay much attention as the others discussed the havoc created in houses, businesses, and in our own store by the swollen waters of the Stoneycreek overflowing its banks in our end of Hollsopple. Eventually, when electricity was restored, the radio brought news of the disastrous conditions in Johnstown as the Little Conemaugh River joined the Stoneycreek in flooding the communities in their paths. At the moment I listened absently, still too caught up in my own misery about the playhouse to be much concerned about other local losses.

Finally, after helping to clear the table and do the dishes, I became interested in the talk about the sleeping arrangements. Mother let us find our pajamas in the suitcase and change clothes in Sister's bedroom. We thought this was fun, but the big question to me was who was going to get to sleep on the studio couch, a fascinating new piece of furniture that opened out into a double bed with a thin mattress. I had been longing to spend a night at Sister's, sleeping on the opened-out couch, but now it looked as though Mother and Daddy would probably sleep there, with the rest of us blanketed on the floor. And that's the way it turned out that Tuesday night, and for the next ten days or so until the flood waters receded and the streets dried up and people returned to their homes.

Every day our dad went down into Hollsopple, and the firemen took him to the store so he could check on things. He'd return in just an hour or two because the dampness was hard on his asthma. One day Daddy noticed that Mr. Bruno was inside his shop cleaning up stuff, so the next day he took my flappy shoe with him and left it to be repaired. He was able to return it to me in a couple of days, to my relief, for I had been hobbling around, half shod.

Other than for occasional brief ventures outside for a breath of fresh air, the rest of us stayed in the small apartment and read, played games, cooked, and ate meals. We worked at our lessons with Jeanne as the teacher. We played store, taking turns as the clerk. Sister drew pictures for us, gave us art lessons, and made the most beautiful paper dolls. Jeanne and I sang all the songs we could remember from our chorus repertoire. Mother sang old songs, like "Babes in the Woods," that she had learned as a child from her sister, Aunt Lizzie, who had played the organ in silent movie theaters.

I memorized several poems by Robert Louis Stevenson, including "The Land of Counterpane," about a sick child who lies in bed playing with small lead soldiers, marching them up and down the hills that his knees made under the blanket. Stevenson was my favorite poet, since we had learned "Where Go the Boats?" earlier in the year, as second-graders had for years. The first verse, "Dark brown is the river/ Golden is the sand/ It flows along for ever/ With trees on either hand," had seemed a perfect description of the Stoneycreek as it placidly wound its way around our town. Now I had mixed feelings toward the once-benign stream that had left its pleasant banks to disrupt the life of our family and the townspeople, not just for the immediate future, I was to discover, but for years to come.

Every day Dad came back with new stories he had heard, mainly from the firemen and fellows from the Civilian Conservation Corps, who were doing what they could to clean up the town, hauling away broken-up sheds and outhouses and other stuff that couldn't be reused. In the early days after the flood they had strung a heavy rope across the beginning of our street to keep homeowners from trying to get back into their homes too soon. Along the length of the short gravel road the force of the flood had washed holes, gulches, and gullies, which filled with the dirty brown water and created real safety hazards. In addition, sidewalks were dislodged and pushed up at dangerous angles. People pleaded in vain to be allowed to go to check on their properties and to retrieve valuable items. One of them,

Mr. Helsel, who lived at the very end of the street, nearest to the river, had recently been hospitalized. He finally gave up and just hung on to the rope and cried at the thought of the damage his house was suffering.

Another really incredible story concerned Mrs. Helsel and her wedding ring, which she had lost in 1908 in the yard of the house she and her family had lived in over on Whistler Street. When they moved to our street, Mrs. Helsel told the new owners, the Zbrozeks, about the lost ring, how it had flown off her finger when she back-handed one of the kids. The Zbrozeks promised to keep an eye out for it. So, there they were in 1936, trying to clean up the yard from all the debris of their demolished barn (they lost their cow, car, and chickens!), when one of them spied something shiny in the muddy grass. Sure enough, when the mud was polished away from inside the gold band, there were the initials, *MDH~TEA,* and the date of their wedding, *4-6-06.* I could just imagine how elated sixteen-year-old Sophie Zbrozek was to tell Mrs. Helsel about the miraculous recovery of her ring after twenty-eight years. I was *so* jealous. I *yearned* to find a long-lost treasure for someone.

One day Dad told us a funny thing about bars of Ivory soap he had found floating all over the store, their white and blue wrappers loosened and dirty. All the canned goods on low shelves had lost their labels. For a long time afterward Mother served us "flood surprises," vegetables or fruit that came from unmarked cans unable to be sold because their contents were unpredictable. Unfortunately, many foods were unusable, such as the bulk dried beans and rice that soaked and swelled in the dirty flood waters.

Every day Daddy brought home the *Johnstown Tribune* or *Democrat*, sometimes both, and we read all the flood news and cut out articles and pictures to save for a scrapbook. Most of the stories concerned Johnstown, since it was a much larger town, but we were disappointed that Hollsopple wasn't mentioned more. Of course, the damage done by our one river couldn't compare with that caused by the three in Johnstown overflowing their banks. Gwen listened to the discussions and even understood some of the news.

"You mean that our river went on to Johnstown and made another flood there?" she demanded, as though disappointed in a friend. Dad explained about the Stoneycreek meeting up with the Little Conemaugh and creating the Conemaugh River.

"You know how much fun you had this winter with all that snow?" he asked.

"Yeah," I said, "it never seemed to go away. We just kept getting more and more snow. It was really good for sledriding." I thought sadly of our vanished sleds and the exhilarating rides down Radabushes' hill.

"That's right," our father continued, "and that's where the big problem began." We looked at him but didn't say anything, just waited. "Do you remember last weekend when it suddenly warmed up?" We nodded. "Well, all that snow started melting in the hills around here and running into the rivers. And then what happened?"

"It started to rain," Jeanne said, "and the rivers couldn't hold that much water."

"The water all piled up!" exclaimed Gwen. "And then it spilled over!"

Our dad would have made a good teacher. He liked to read about things in the paper, look them up in our encyclopedias, and discuss news with us. For instance, he pointed out the item about the Johnstown Inclined Plane carrying four thousand people up to safety in Westmont, a residential section of the city. "Did you know that it was built after the 1889 flood for just that purpose?" We didn't. Grandma Reese had told us about the earlier flood that had claimed over two thousand lives and about the South Fork Dam's breaking. We hadn't realized that it was considered the worst natural disaster in the U. S. until the San Francisco earthquake.[1]

Somehow, since Mother had been born in 1889 and our dad's family lived in South Fork, we felt a certain connection to the '89 flood, so we decided that sometime after Johnstown was cleaned up, we'd go there and ride the Incline. We just lived ten miles away, so it wouldn't take long to get there.

When the newspapers reported that Johnstown had had twelve deaths and nine thousand people made homeless, we realized that Hollsopple, despite a lot of property damage, had fortunately escaped with no fatalities, and most of our people eventually were able to return to homes more or less intact.

Another newspaper story was memorable because it covered a rumor, not an actual event. The day after the flood, March 18, a pilot flying in a small aircraft around the area saw water spilling over the breast of the Quemahoning Dam, south of Hollsopple, and jumped to the conclusion that the dam had burst. He returned to Johnstown and frantically began to warn everyone to head for the hills. In the attempt to reach safety many people ran, exhausted and desperate, dragging and carrying family members up the hillsides. Tragically, one woman had a heart attack and died as she tried to escape from the false threat.

Later, we heard that a friend of ours, Betty Blough, had also been affected by the same rumor. On the day of the flood she came home from high school in Johnstown, and because she couldn't get across the bridge, she stayed overnight on the other side with a girlfriend. The next day when the warning came about the dam breaking, Betty and her friend grabbed the friend's mother, one at each arm, and started to run toward Davidsville, the older woman crying and babbling in broken English. They ran and ran, Betty didn't remember exactly how far, until they couldn't go any farther. They stopped to rest and finally realized that they were not in any danger. Eventually, they walked back home alongside many others, embarrassed but relieved that the crisis had not been real. It wasn't long before radio announcements dispelled the rumor.

After about a week our father came home with an unbelievable bit of news: A fireman who had gone to see the flood damage in Johnstown told him that he was positive he had seen our playhouse washed up several miles away along the course of the Stoneycreek. As the water went down, the little house had simply come to rest and had stayed.

"Oh, Daddy, do you really think it's ours? Can we get it back?" I almost cried. You can imagine the hope that was stirred up when Dad told us that he would drive the next day to that area and talk to the property owners about retrieving the playhouse.

He took with him a snapshot of Denny and me in front of the playhouse, showing clearly the size of the building, the distinctive little windows, and the shingled roof. After he left, we kept telling each other joyfully that we *hadn't* lost the playhouse. After all, the picture proved that we were the original owners.

Several hours later when he returned to the boarding house, one look at his tired, sad face broke the unhappy news that he was unsuccessful. "Was it our playhouse, Daddy?" we asked as he sat down at the table. He simply nodded.

"Did you show them the picture?"
"Yes."

"Didn't they believe that it was the same?" I demanded.

"Oh, yes," he replied, "the man said it definitely looked the same."

"Well, is he going to give it back?"

"No, he isn't."

"Why not?!" We were incredulous. How could this be?

"Because he doesn't have to." Dad sighed before he went on. "The man said he had checked with his lawyer about things that were washed up from the flood, and the lawyer told him that, legally, he could keep anything that remained on his property. It's the law of salvage, he said."

"How can that be right, Daddy," asked Jeanne, "when it's *our* playhouse?"

"I know it doesn't seem right, but I checked and it *is* the law," he answered. "I think I have to lie down for a little while, okay?" He got up and went over to the couch and lay down. "I'm sorry, kids." We wanted to ask him more about it, but Mother shook her head at us and covered him with an afghan. He closed his eyes and seemed to fall asleep, but I looked at him now and then and saw wet marks on his cheeks. He really feels bad about the playhouse, I thought.

Eventually the water went down, and we kids tramped around in the muck, enjoying the noisy, messy sucking at our boots. Then the streets dried up, and people got their homes scrubbed out with the aid of the CCC. Damp, muddy cellars with rotting fruits and vegetables from broken jars and storage bins demanded immediate attention because of health concerns. Rugs and furniture had to be cleaned or discarded. New outhouses were arranged for and delivered; amazingly, we got one! (Gwen deliberately found occasion to use it, too.)

We returned to a backyard that felt unfamiliar and empty: no garage, grape arbor, chicken coop, back or side steps, and, most painful to us children, no playhouse. A snowfall in early April left us feeling quite deprived: no sleds.

I had thought, that Tuesday, that the water would simply go down and everything would go back to normal. On the surface, perhaps, it seemed to do so. However, stresses from the flood, added to those of the Depression, caused upheaval in our lives more significant than dislodged sidewalks, resulting in our dad's gradually deteriorating health and the bankruptcy of the store.

But not right away, nor all at once.

10

WHEN DREAMS OF CAMPING DIE

"I'm going home," I announced.

"Good!" said Thelma Shaffer. "'Cause I hate you."

Her statement stopped me at the door. No one had ever said that to me before. And all because of the Sears catalog.

Since our dad owned the general store in Hollsopple, most of our family's buying needs were satisfied at the store, so we never had a catalog of any kind in our home. Things were different across the yard at the Shaffers' house, since all their friends and relatives with inside bathrooms gave them their old catalogs. The oldest copies were sent to the outhouse, the newest ones were kept for ordering, while the ones in between were used for cut-outs and playing.

For a while we played a simple game of just leafing through the pages and picking things we liked. This eventually evolved into the Hundred Dollar Game, in which we each pretended to have exactly that amount of money to spend, and our order had to come within one dollar of the hundred-dollar limit, without going over. Sometimes we picked things just for ourselves, but now and then we generously included things for the rest of our families. Toys and clothes were the most popular choices for both Thelma and me for a long time. Gradually, however, I began to tire of Shirley Temple and Dionne quintuplet dolls, games, and fur-trimmed coats and muffs, and started flipping pages to unfamiliar merchandise.

That's when I discovered camping equipment.

Although John and Bob had gone camping with the Boy Scouts, none of the rest of us had any knowledge of the activity. At first, I merely added a pup tent or a Coleman lantern to my order to help the total reach one hundred dollars. Little by little, however, outdoor supplies began to edge out clothes and toys. Thelma noticed this shopping trend and casually started to follow suit. By the time I was picking out deluxe family tents for four kids (Sister was married, and John was working, so I figured they wouldn't be able to go camping) plus two parents, Thelma was buying double sleeping bags "so everybody could stay warm."

Two or three days a week after school that fall when I was in fifth grade, I hurried over to the Shaffer house and made out a fake order for camping equipment. I was now adding hiking clothes and rain gear for active outdoor sports, plus sturdy, all-weather shoes and knapsacks. There was only one problem: everything I chose, all my unique discoveries, from practical tinware for outdoor meals to ice chests for keeping food cold, *everything* was copied faithfully by Thelma, and this was beginning to annoy me.

Finally, one afternoon, after Thelma listened to my list and happily declared, "I'm going to order exactly the same things for my family," I put my foot down.

"I don't think we should be allowed to order exactly the same things as the other person," I objected.

"Why not?" asked Thelma. "It's not like we're going to run out of stuff."

"I know, but," I tried to think of a reason, "it's not fair when I find the things to order and add up all the prices, and then you just order the same stuff."

"But what if I like it?"

"You shouldn't be able to like exactly what I like," I argued. "We should have rules."

"We're just pretending," Thelma reminded me. "Why should you be able to make rules about what I pretend?"

That's when I decided to go home, and Thelma told me that she hated me. "Why are you so mad at me?" I asked her.

"Because you always want to run everything," she said in a funny voice.

"I do not!" I protested. I looked for support at Beattie and Lorraine, Thelma's sisters, and then at Denny, my sister. Nobody said anything. "I just get ideas, that's all," I tried to explain. "I thought you liked my ideas."

"You always think your ideas are the best," replied Thelma, "just because you're rich!"

My mouth fell open. "We're not rich!" I protested.

"Yes, you are," she shot back. "You have a car."

"You have an inside toilet," added Beattie. Lorraine nodded agreement.

"But we have an outside one, too," Gwen offered brightly, although surprised at my frown. It was true. For some reason I never understood, after the flood we had requested and received an outhouse just like the others on our street.

"You always have real bathing suits to swim in, not just old clothes," Thelma continued with her litany of our richness.

"Thelma," I tried to explain, "they're not new. They always come from someone else. Sometimes Mother has to mend the holes before we can wear them. I don't know why you think we're rich."

Lorraine spoke for the first time. "You have a daddy."

I barely glanced at her. "That doesn't make us rich."

"When he has a store, it does," countered Thelma. Her sisters chimed in, "Yeah."

Beattie continued, "You can go there anytime and get what you want, free. *That's rich.*"

"We can*not!*" I turned to Gwen. "Can we, Denny?"

"Oh, no!" she exclaimed with enthusiasm. "Except sometimes if I ask Daddy if I can have a sucker, he says, 'Okay, get it out of the candy case.'" A second frown from me stopped her short. "What?"

I couldn't think of any other arguments and just stood there looking at them, then turned to go. My hand was on the doorknob when Thelma's next remark stopped me again.

"Well, even if you're rich now, our ma says it won't be for long."

"What do you mean?" I let go of the knob and turned back to her. "What do you mean, Thelma?"

She seemed a little hesitant now that I was confronting her. "Ma says that your dad is going to lose the store again. There's going to be a big sale."

I glared at her and went back and grabbed Gwen's hand. "Let's go home, Denny." We went out the door, down the steps, and across the yard to our own house without talking. I can't believe it, I thought. Daddy's going to lose the store again. After the flood, when the store had gone bankrupt and Dad Bailey left the partnership, our father had gotten the store cleaned up and borrowed money to start up again, changing the name from JIMANDAD'S to JIM'S FAMILY STORE. He had worked so hard the last two years to keep the new store going, his health had really suffered. I couldn't stand the thought of the darkened store and the quiet, unmoving little payment cups.

"Just in time to set the table, girls," Mother greeted us as we entered the kitchen. "Get down the soup bowls; we're having *chili con carne.*"

Just then John and Bob came bursting in from their twenty-mile drive from Somerset, where John was working in the Turnpike office and Bob was a senior in high school. Did they know about the store, I wondered.

We had supper the same as usual, with everyone talking and laughing, even Daddy now and then. It can't be true, I thought. Am I the only one who knows? I didn't say anything about the store then, but while we were cleaning up after the meal, I decided to see whether Mother would talk about it. However, she seemed reluctant.

"Mother, is it true we're going to lose the store again?"

"I don't know, Ruth. We hope not." She paused before continuing. "Were they talking about the store at the Shaffers'?"

"A little," I hedged, finding myself as reticent as my mother. "Thelma's mother says there's going to be a big sale. Is there?"

"It just depends."

"On what?"

"Well," Mother replied (sadly? cynically? hopefully? I wasn't sure), "it depends on whether the people who owe us money will try to pay us."

"Do you think they will?" I asked her.

"I really don't know, honey. A lot of them are friends, so maybe they will. One way or the other, we'll know in a couple of weeks, so there's no point in worrying about it now." I could tell she was finished talking about it, so I started running water into the dishpan and watched the soap bubbles frothing up and then collapsing. Frothing up and then collapsing.

For some reason camping equipment lost its appeal for me, as did make-believe orders from the Sears catalog. We never played that game again.

11

LITTLE JIMMY AND THE GREAT FALL OF CHINA

Of all the things that our sister Elizabeth did for Gwen and me—making clothes, drawing pictures, creating paper dolls, playing the piano, teaching us songs, telling stories, babysitting endlessly—the absolute best was making AUNTS out of us!

When I was nine and Gwen was seven, out of the blue, it seemed to us, Sister had a baby boy. We had not noticed the change in her shape nor heard any talk of the coming event, so we were completely charmed by the unexpected arrival. Both his grandfathers were named Jim and his father was called Jimmy, and since the name was to be passed on, he became Little Jimmy to us.

Some of our friends had younger brothers and sisters, but we were the only aunts. Aunts walked babies in carriages up and down the sidewalk (don't cross the road), and later, in strollers (don't walk too fast). Aunts sat by babies sleeping on the swing, sang little songs to try to keep them from crying, and played "This little piggy went to market" to make them laugh. Oh, that gurgly, happy laugh, that most winsome of sounds! And the announcement "Here comes Sister with Little Jimmy!" was enough to transform the dreariest, most boring day.

We were awaiting their arrival one Sunday in early December when our nephew was about seventeen months old. In honor of company we were going to eat in the dining room instead of the kitchen, so Jeanne was assigned to oversee the setting of the table. Gwen was dispatched to get our regular silverware from the kitchen, while I got the everyday dishes. After I had set out all the plates, cups, and saucers, I started looking for the extra pieces I liked especially.

"Jeanne, can we use the rose bowls for the mashed potatoes and the dressing?" I asked as I held one of the large fragile bowls hand-painted in bright shades of deep red, rose, and pink. It had belonged to Grandma Mugridge.

"No, not for something hot. The applesauce or coleslaw, okay," she replied. I took the bowls carefully out to the kitchen table and came back to the china cabinet. I knew which pieces I wanted now: the two cow cream pitchers, one black and white, one red and white, one from each of our grandmothers. The cows were regarding me placidly from the eye-level shelf directly in front of me.

"Jeanne, can we use both cow creamers?" She was arranging the plates and stopped to consider my question. Before she could answer, I quickly added, "One for each end of the table. They won't have to be filled again, and they won't have to be passed so much. Okay? Please?" She paused, then smiled and said okay.

By the time the table was all set, we heard voices and steps at the back door along with Gwen's announcement. There was a lot of laughing, talking, greeting the baby, and just general noise until Mother told everyone to get to the table and the food was brought in.

It was so nice to have our whole family there. In addition to our parents, one at each end, there was Uncle Will, Mother's oldest brother, separating John and Bob on one side. Sister and Jimmy sat on the other side with Little Jimmy in the well-worn family high-chair. Gwen, as usual, was sitting as close as she could to the baby.

Jeanne and I sat on either side of Mother because Daddy had a rule that he tried to enforce: Once we brought everything to the table and Mother sat down, she was not to get up to go to the kitchen for anything. "There are enough kids for that," he insisted. Most of the time it worked, like today, with Jeanne and me going for refills of mashed potatoes, gravy, water, a different kind of jelly, or servings of dessert. What's wrong with boys ever doing that, I grumbled to myself as I brought in a third plate of bread and set it by one of the cow pitchers. At least the cows didn't have to be refilled.

"Mother," began Sister before a squawk from the baby interrupted her. She started again, "I want this cake recipe. I've lost my copy and everyone loves it." Mother's Lady Baltimore cake was well-known in town. However, a squeal from the high chair drowned out comments about the cake.

"Sister," suggested Gwen, "I could ride Little Jimmy around in his stroller if you want me to. He's starting to get fussy, don't you think?"

"Okay, Denny," agreed Sister, "he doesn't want any more to eat, so maybe he'll go to sleep if you don't bounce him too much." Hmm,

I thought, she should know better. However, things were fairly quiet for a little while, and conversation picked up at the table. Sister brought up something she had mentioned once before: the right front leg of the china cabinet. "I thought you were going to have someone tighten that leg, Mother, weren't you?"

"Mr. Helsel is going to pick up the cabinet on Tuesday to work on it," Mother replied. "In fact, you can help me take everything out of it this afternoon and pack it in boxes if you want to."

Maybe I'll help, too, I thought. I really liked to look at old pitchers and dishes that had belonged to our grandmothers and hear Mother talk about where they had come from. Like the two cow creamers on the table and the different colored glass bowls that sometimes were included in boxes of soap powder or given as bingo prizes.

"Back to the cake recipe, Beth," Daddy put in. "Don't you have that little recipe book that we made up at the store? I thought I gave you one."

"Oh, you did, Dad," replied Sister. "It's very popular. In fact, it's so popular that it's disappeared." Everybody laughed.

"Oh, I just remembered," said Mother, "you won't have to make a copy of my recipe. Your daddy put it in this week's paper. Just a minute, I'll get it for you." She got up to go out to the kitchen and almost bumped into Gwen rushing through the swinging door with the stroller. "Not so fast, honey. You might scare Little Jimmy."

"Oh, he likes to go fast!" laughed Gwen as she hurried through the dining room and out the hall door to the living room, with the baby pounding the tray and chortling in excitement. "He's not at all sleepy." How could he be, I thought.

Mother returned almost immediately with the store paper, a sales flyer that our dad typed, mimeographed, and distributed every Thursday. He included news items from the churches and town organizations, and jokes and witty sayings, in addition to selected recipes from the town's best cooks. "I didn't know whether you had this copy yet or not." She paused. "It might be the last issue." The rest of us were satisfied to eat the delicious white cake, while Mother and Sister discussed its fine points, the question about the paper's future and that of the store hovering unspoken around us.

All of a sudden the swinging door banged open and the stroller bumped recklessly through, Gwen and Little Jimmy laughing and squealing. "Slow down, Gwen!" Daddy called out firmly. She glanced over at him, suddenly aware of the reproach and warning in his voice, and at that moment the right front wheel of the stroller hit the problem leg of the china cabinet. I saw the look of horror on Gwen's face as she turned to see the piece of furniture as it wobbled, hesitated, and wavered as though making a decision. She threw her right arm up to ward off the heavy glass and wood cabinet, bracing herself against it, and in the last instant, gave the stroller a mighty push out of the way and shrieked as the cabinet made up its mind and fell on top of her. The stroller jarred into the wall, and the baby started to cry.

Probably no more than four or five seconds had elapsed between the initial impact of the stroller and the splintering crash as the cabinet spilled its contents onto Gwen and the floor. The sounds of screaming, crying, and glass shattering seemed to paralyze me but not the others at the table. Sister and Jimmy ran for their baby, while the others rushed to move the cabinet off Gwen. I had to turn my eyes away from the huge splatters of blood on her face and dress, but Mother fell to her knees and tried to gather Gwen close to her, blood and all.

"John," said Daddy in a quiet voice, "can you pick her up? I'll start the car. Mary, you get your coat. Bob, run up to the linen closet and get an old blanket. We won't try to put her coat on." He got his coat from the hall closet and went out the back door.

John stooped down and easily took Gwen from Mother's arms and stood up. Bob was back already with an old quilt, which he draped around her. Mother buttoned her coat, spoke to Sister about taking charge of things, and hurried out the door after John.

I still hadn't moved from my chair at the table. They'll be at the doctor's in a few minutes, I thought, and she'll be okay. I looked down at the mess of broken glass, china and spatters of blood; then I stood up and with the toe of my shoe turned over a broken plate: one of mother's good dishes. I glanced around. There wasn't a single whole plate left, but several unbroken pairs of salt and pepper shakers from the good set were huddled together like orphans. Some heavy cut glass pieces from the bottom shelf had survived intact, probably because they hadn't fallen very far. I looked over at the clock on the buffet. They're at the doctor's by now, I thought, and she'll be okay, I know she'll be okay.

Little Jimmy had quieted down by then so his father was holding him while Sister organized the cleanup. "If there's anything broken in just a couple of pieces, maybe we can mend it. Otherwise, we might as well just sweep up everything else into these two boxes," she said. Bob started picking up the bigger pieces, putting them into one of the boxes. Jeanne went to get the broom and dustpan.

I stood looking at the table. "Ruth," said Sister, "why don't you take the dirty dishes to the kitchen? We can all help do them as soon as we have the broken pieces cleaned up." I said okay but didn't move. I just looked at the black and white cow creamer and then at the red and white one at the other end of the table. I saved them, I thought. I used them on the table, along with the rose bowls. Otherwise, they'd be broken, too. Mother will be glad to know that some things she really likes survived.

"Well," said Bob, "I guess this saves us packing all the stuff from the china closet for the big move."

"You mean for Mr. Helsel?" I asked him, carrying a stack of dishes to the door.

"No, I mean for the big move to Somerset."

"What are you talking about?" I demanded.

He straightened up. "If we lose the store, we'll have to move," he answered.

This was a new thought for me. "Why?"

"When Daddy borrowed money to start up the store again," Bob explained, "he had to put up the house as collateral." He saw my confusion and continued. "That means if he can't pay off the loan for the store, the house has to be sold."

"But that doesn't mean we're moving to Somerset," I protested. I looked to Jeanne for support. "Why can't we find another house here in Hollsopple?"

"Because John has a job in Somerset, that's why," Jeanne said. "I think he's already found a house for us to rent there in case they don't get enough money for the store."

Bob nodded. "We went past it the other day before we drove home. It's pretty nice." For over a year he had been riding to Somerset with John and attending high school there while John worked in the Turnpike office.[1]

I couldn't believe all this. Why hadn't they told Gwen and me about moving? We knew that Dad might lose the store, but it had happened before, and he had simply started up again. Why didn't they tell us about it?

Jeanne seemed to understood what I was feeling. "I think they didn't want to worry you two in case everything turns out okay and we don't have to move."

"Well," I grumbled, "I don't think we should have to move. All our friends are here. We don't know anyone in Somerset."

"I know," said Jeanne, "but Ruth, you have to understand, there's nothing that they can do about it. People simply owe the store too much money."

"I don't know why they won't pay it," I complained. "*We* need the money, too."

"I heard Daddy tell Mother something," Bob confided. "He said that if 350 people would pay just ten dollars of what they owe, we could keep the house *and* the store."

That didn't sound too bad to me. "Maybe they *will* pay," I said hopefully. "Maybe we won't have to move."

Sister had been listening all along without saying anything but now seemed to feel she had to settle the matter. "Don't count on it, honey. People are really having a hard time everywhere. The Depression still isn't over."

I just stopped talking and concentrated on clearing the table of the dirty dishes. Finally, I came back and sat down again. I moved the two cows and the rose bowls around in different patterns, wondering what Mother would think to see the few unbroken survivors and the badly battered china cabinet. The cows faced each other and mooed in a friendly way. "Moo," replied Little Jimmy, reaching up to be held. "Moooo!"

I couldn't resist the little flexing hands and appealing eyes and pulled him up on my lap. I let each cow approach him and converse briefly, but when he wanted to handle them himself, I put him down and took the cows over to the safety of the buffet. I didn't want anything to happen to them. I took him to the living room and sat on the floor with him and Jeanne, rolling a ball back and forth to him, all of us waiting and listening for the return of the car.

"They're coming," reported Bob from his lookout at the window over the sofa. "Here they are."

We were all waiting in the kitchen at the back door when they arrived. John was still carrying Gwen, all bundled up in the old quilt with just her eyes and bandaged nose showing. He set her down on the linoleum and removed the quilt. She hopped to a chair and sat down.

"Ruth," she announced excitedly through puffy lips, "I lost my shoe! If I can't find it, Daddy says I can get a new pair. It didn't even have a hole in it!" She looked around in surprise when everyone laughed, relieved. "Where's Little Jimmy?" she asked. "Is he okay?"

At her voice he called out "Den!" and struggled to get out of Sister's arms. She let him run over to Gwen, but he stopped suddenly when he saw her bruised, bandaged face.

"It's *me*, honey," she said, speaking as clearly as she could. "You know me." He reached out to touch her nose, but Sister pulled him back before he made contact.

"I don't want him to hurt you, Denny. He might be rough," cautioned Sister. "Just wait a little while and he'll be okay." Gwen nodded in agreement, then thought of something else.

"I want to see the china closet. Is it all broken?" she asked, getting to her feet in a gingerly way.

"You better not walk in there in your sock foot," Jeanne advised. "There still might be some little pieces of glass on the floor."

Mother interrupted, "Gwen, I want you to go lie down on the sofa. The doctor said you have to rest."

"Just this one thing and I'll lie down," coaxed Gwen.

"All right," Mother gave in, "just this one thing."

Gwen pointed at the mat by the door. "Bring me one of my artics, okay? I'll just wear that." So, wearing one shoe and one boot and leaning on Bob, she hobbled into the dining room and inspected the disabled cabinet, lying empty on its back. All of us trailed after her, wanting somehow to comfort her but feeling a little at a loss at the sight of the empty wall. "Is everything all broke?" she asked at last.

Happy to answer her, I sprang into action. "Look, Denny, on the buffet! The cows!"

She turned, saw the cream pitchers, and started to beam. "And the rose bowls, too!" she marveled. "And, Mother, look! Your good salt and pepper shakers—your favorites!"

"And all those heavy glass pieces," I added, "it's really good that they were saved. They're just about your...your..." I hesitated to use the word I wanted, "your most precious stuff, isn't that right?"

Mother leaned over to pick up Little Jimmy before she answered me. "No," she said, shifting him to her right hip and pulling Gwen near, "no, that's not right, Ruth. It's not even close." She leaned forward awkwardly because her arms were full and kissed my cheek before she repeated, "It's not even close."

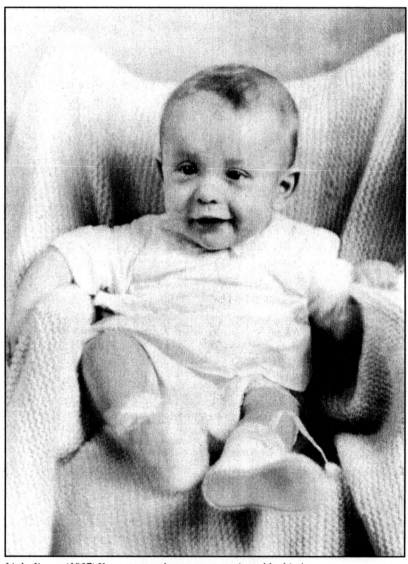

Little Jimmy (1937) You can see why we were captivated by him!
Photo courtesy of Marcy Zeppernick

12

THE LAST CHAPTER

When something is almost over, when it's almost finished, when you're not going to do it or see it or have it anymore and *you know it,* I think you should take the time to…well, say goodbye to it.

It was Monday morning before school. I sat on the edge of my bed just thinking about things. It was going to be a busy week, with four days left of school before vacation started on Friday. Christmas was going to be on Sunday, and we would be moving on Monday or Tuesday. This meant a lot of rushing for us, but Mother thought it would be good to be all settled in Somerset before school started again in January.

I think, in a way, since we *had* to move, Mother just wanted to get it over with as soon as possible.

I picked up my hairbrush and started to brush my hair. I thought of Grandma Reese, who had died the summer after the flood while staying with Uncle Jim and Aunt Gertie in Houtzdale. She had fallen and broken her hip, and although Mother and Gwen spent several weeks with her before the end, the rest of us had to be satisfied with going to the funeral.

I remembered so many mornings sitting here on the bed beside Grandma, taking turns with Gwen at brushing her long white hair. She would roll up the strands that she removed from her brush and place the little ball outside on the ledge. "Watch, now," she would say, and we'd wait for just a minute or so until a little brown bird flew down to the window, picked up the ball of hair, and flew away. I had always enjoyed the thought of Grandma's soft white hair helping to line a little bird's nest and make it cozy and warm.

"Ruth," called Gwen from the stairs, "Mother says to hurry or you'll be late."

I went down for a quick breakfast and Gwen and I soon left for school. I was glad that we were busy all day so that I didn't have to think about moving. After school, when I met Gwen outside, I suggested going to the store.

"What for?" she asked.

At first I just shrugged, but finally I said, "This is the last day the store is open, Denny. The sale's tomorrow. Don't you want to see the store one last time?"

"Oh, sure," she agreed.

We looked around for our father in all the departments on the first floor, starting with the shoe room, where cleared shelves and a scattering of boxes reflected Dad's decision months before to stop reordering sizes and new styles. Next, we studied the few remaining colorful bolts of material, which we loved because Sister had always let us have our choices for the dresses she made for us, which usually took between one and two yards apiece at 29–39 cents a yard. We hardly gave a glance at sparse displays of underwear and long brown cotton stockings. Without stopping, we passed the display cases that once held candy bars, gum, and penny candy and glanced back through the empty produce aisles and over grocery counters.

"Are you going to buy something?" Gwen finally asked, curiosity winning out after we had wandered through all the departments, finally stopping at the raised, open office in the center. Romaine looked up from her books and smiled.

"Looking for your dad?" she asked, and when we nodded, she pointed upwards with her pen. We thanked her and headed toward the back, where the stairs were located. I noticed on the way that the meat cases were completely, starkly clean.

All this emptiness, I thought, as we walked upstairs. I found myself wishing that I had allowed my last memory of the store to be one of busyness and cheerful clerks and customers, rather than this feeling of being disconnected. The second floor, once stocked with small farm and lawn equipment and toys such as tricycles, bicycles, scooters, and sleds, was practically deserted. Daddy must have been taking a break because he was sitting on a box, not doing anything. "Did you come up for a ride?" he asked. "You're in luck. There are two scooters left. You'll have lots of room." He pointed over at a small collection of kids' things against the wall. He always let us play with some of the stuff when he was working up there.

Gwen went over right away and picked up a scooter and pushed off, heading for the far end of the second floor. At home we had only one scooter, which we had to take turns on, so this would have been a good chance to race with Gwen, but I just stood there, wishing I could think of something to say. "It looks different," I finally mumbled, "empty."

He cleared his throat and nodded. We watched Gwen flying past. "I'll race you!" she called back over her shoulder.

"You'd better get your ride," he said. "I'm going to have to turn off the lights and go downstairs in a few minutes. I told your mother I'd be home early for supper."

"You don't have to wait, Daddy," I told him. "I'll just be a couple of minutes. I can turn off the lights when we go down." I picked up the other scooter and waited while Gwen was approaching.

"That's okay," he answered. "I don't mind waiting. I'm all finished downstairs." So he sat there while Gwen and I rode around the empty storeroom. The second time, I looked over at him from across the floor and saw him kind of rub his hands over his face, but when we slowed down and stopped at the box, he stood up and was halfway smiling at us. "Well," he said as we started down the steps, "that was a nice way to say goodbye to the store, wasn't it?" He motioned to me to turn out the lights.

He knew what I was doing.

As we passed one of the grocery counters, I pointed at one of the little money cups and he nodded his okay. I reached up and pulled the cord and sent the cup swinging on overhead wires to the office. Of course, since Romaine had left already, no one was there to send it back. Since Gwen wanted her turn, I stepped up into the office and pulled the cord, returning the money cup to where she was waiting. She boosted herself up onto the counter and took hold of the handle and pulled hard. It always tickled us to see a little cup sailing so busily throughout the store, carrying payments, receipts, and change, but empty and purposeless, it didn't seem as much fun as it usually had. We turned out the rest of the lights and went out the front door. Dad locked it and we went home, crunching through the snow and not talking about much of anything.

That night, I got up after a couple of hours of sleep to go to the bathroom and was passing my parents' half-open bedroom door when I heard a funny sound, something like a moan that ended in a sob. Oh, I thought, stifling a sob myself, Mother's crying. I wanted to push open the door and go and comfort her but stopped, stunned, when I heard her calm voice. "Jim," she said, "Jim, wake up."

The strange sound stopped. "I'm not asleep," I heard my father say. I tiptoed away and went to the bathroom. On the way back to my room, as I passed their door, I heard low murmurs but I couldn't understand what they were saying.

The next morning we got up and ate breakfast and went to school, and Bob and John left for Somerset as usual. That evening at supper we learned that the house had been sold to pay the debt on the store. "How much did the house sell for?" John asked.

Dad looked at Mother, who shrugged as if to say, *You might as well tell them.* "Thirty-five hundred," he answered quietly.

"That's the exact amount you needed," said John angrily. I didn't understand his tone. He went on, "It sounds as though someone knew exactly the amount to bid."

"There was just one bid," Mother put in flatly, "and since that's all they needed, that's where they stopped." She didn't seem to want to talk any more about the sale. In a few minutes she started gathering the dishes, and Gwen, Jeanne, and I got up to help her. Bob, John, and Uncle Will went into the living room to pack up boxes of books.

I glanced at Dad sitting at the table by himself, his head resting in his hand. I thought of the strange sounds I had heard the night before and had a sudden vision of what life was going to be like in Somerset. We would all be missing friends. The new school would probably be so different from our little three-room one in Hollsopple, where the teachers knew everyone's family, and our father was on the school board and every other board in town. Jeanne and I wouldn't be singing in the children's choir anymore, I thought with a pang. That's just about the worst thing. No, I changed my mind, not being able to play outside with the other kids in the neighborhood, that's the worst. Then I thought of the river, of not being able to swim at Butcher Hole. That's it, I thought. That's the worst.

"No," I said out loud and stopped when the others looked at me. "Nothing," I mumbled. "I was thinking of something."

I took the dish towel Jeanne was holding out to me and started drying dishes. I had been about to say that the worst thing was not having good times in this house with the rest of the family. We're probably all going to be real sad from now on, especially Daddy. As though sensing that I was thinking about him, he pushed his chair back from the table and got up.

"That was a good supper, Mother," he said as usual. "I think I'm going to go to bed early tonight."

"That's a good idea," she answered, turning from the sink slightly to nod at him. "You've had a hard day."

After finishing the dishes, we helped Mother pack some pots and pans in orange crates and brought a bunch of the jars of canned food up from the cellar so they could be packed the next day. It wasn't long before everybody decided to turn in early.

"Mother, where's Daddy?" I asked the next morning at breakfast.

"He went to Somerset with John and Bob," she answered. "He had to go to the courthouse to take care of some business about the store and the house. Why?"

"I just wondered," I said. "What's he going to do all day while he waits for them?" I hated the thought of his being alone, tired and sad in a strange town.

"He'll be okay, Ruth," she reassured me. "He's going to the bank and the post office, and I think maybe the school. If he gets tired, he can go to our new house. John's been taking things there every day. When he gets hungry, he might go to a restaurant the Spanglers told him about that's near Somerset. Their son Fred is married to the sister of the owner. Oakhurst Tea Room,[1] I think its name is." Mother handed me my bowl of hot oatmeal. "Are you worried about him?" When I halfway shrugged, she rested her hand on my shoulder briefly and said again, "He'll be okay. He just needs a good rest after all this worry."

I was glad we were busy all day at school, finishing lessons, making paper chains for Christmas trees, and practicing songs and poems for our Christmas program the next day. Our fifth grade had a geography test over the Middle Atlantic states, and when we had all turned our papers in, the teacher announced something about studying the New England states after we came back from Christmas vacation, and I thought, Yeah, without me. I think everybody knew we were going to move, but nobody was saying anything.

Gwen went straight home after school, but I went to the church for rehearsal for the children's choir. We were going to perform at the Christmas Eve service, and it would be the last time for Jeanne and me to sing with the group. Jeanne arrived late as usual with the other girls who attended the new high school at Davidsville. They slipped into place without a word and began to sing the "Coventry Carol" the second time through with us.

"Lullay, Thou little tiny Child, By, by, lully, lullay...O sisters too, how may we do, For to preserve this day...By, by, lully, lullay."

Their added voices, though soft and muted, brought a gentle fullness to the lullaby. My throat seemed to fill with tears or something, and no sound came out. Mr. Border glanced in my direction with a questioning look on his face, so I tried to make myself sing. After rehearsal I got Jeanne to leave fast so that I didn't have to talk to him about what was wrong. He probably knew anyway.

When we got home, Mother and Gwen were packing all the things from the kitchen cupboards that we wouldn't be needing until we got to Somerset, so we helped them until supper was ready. After waiting for a while for the others to arrive from Somerset, we went ahead and sat down to eat the hot stew that had been cooking all day on the back burner.

After a couple of bites we started to talk about Christmas. Mother's idea was just to forget about decorating a tree, since it would go up on Christmas Eve and we would be moving the day after Christmas. Jeanne thought we should wait until we arrived in Somerset and got settled before we put up a tree that day, Monday. Gwen and I didn't care how it happened, we just wanted to have one in both Hollsopple *and* Somerset. I couldn't imagine waking up on Christmas Day without a lighted tree. Or being in Somerset that whole next week without one. With all the other disappointments we were experiencing, that would be too much.

"Mother, it's not as though we have to buy new decorations," I pleaded. "We still have a lot of old ones. It wouldn't cost anything."

The sound of footsteps and voices on the back porch spared Mother the need to continue the argument. "What's for supper?" John called out as he opened the door.

"I'm hungry!" was Bob's greeting.

Dad didn't say anything as he entered, but he was smiling broadly. Even before he took off his coat, he headed for Mother at her end of the table and gave her a hug. "I got every single thing done that I wanted to!" he exclaimed and leaned down to kiss her cheek. She pushed her chair away from the table and stood up to hug him back.

"Now, take off your coat and get washed up," she said, helping him off with his overcoat. Everybody sat down and Mother filled up the serving bowl with more of the bubbly stew. I cut the rest of the loaf of homemade bread, while Jeanne emptied the jar of Mother's home-canned applesauce into the bowl.

"Mmm, my favorites!" declared Dad as he helped himself to everything. We all laughed because that's what he always said, regardless of what Mother cooked. Just as he was about to take a bite, a knock sounded at the back door. He nodded to Bob, who jumped up to open it. Two women stood on the back porch, the younger one carrying a big kettle with a lid on it. We knew both of them really well.

"Hello, Sophie, Mrs. Zbrozek," said Bob, very politely. "Would you like to come in?"

"Hello, Bobby," replied Sophie. "Yes, thank you very much." She was several years older than Bob and was out of school already. She turned to the older woman. "Let's go in, Mom." The two of them stepped inside, and Bob closed the door. Mother and Dad both stood up and went over to the visitors and greeted them.

"Mr. and Mrs. Mugridge," Sophie began rather shyly, "my mother made something for your family. We hope you like it."

Dad took the kettle from Sophie and placed it on the stove. He reached over and lifted the lid, and a tantalizing smell escaped with the steam. "Oh, golompki! My favorite!" exclaimed my father, and the Zbrozeks looked startled and confused when the rest of our family burst out laughing.

Mother reached out and took Mrs. Zbrozek's hand. "A family joke, that's all." She looked in the kettle and turned to the rest of us. "It is a favorite...stuffed cabbage!" We laughed and cheered, as Mrs. Zbrozek somehow understood our joke and smiled at our parents' thanks.

Then in slow, careful English she spoke to them. "I am sorry that you go. You are good man, Mr. Mugridge. You help me in store." She turned to Mother. "Thank you, Mrs. Mugridge, you are kind lady. You give me, my family, chicken soup when I am sick." (At one time, before I was born, our family had lived on Whistler Street, across from the Zbrozeks.) Mrs. Zbrozek continued, "I name my baby Mary Jeanne for your girl." She nodded at Jeanne and repeated, "I am sorry that you go."

"Thank you, Mrs. Zbrozek, thank you, Sophie," said Mother, and

for a few seconds it seemed as though she wanted to say something
else. When she didn't say anything, Mrs. Zbrozek spoke up.

"*Sophia*, not Sophie," Mrs. Zbrozek said apologetically. Sophia
glared at her mother, who was not finished. "People here just say
Sophie, but her name is So*phia*."

"Thank you, Sophia. It's a beautiful name." Dad smiled at her, and
she relaxed.

Then the two women simply hugged. Dad cleared his throat a
couple of times, and they thanked her and Sophia again, and the
Zbrozeks soon left.

All that emotion seemed to have made me hungry all over again.
At first Mother said that we'd save the stuffed cabbage for the next
day, but when a big groan went up, she relented, so we each had a
small bundle from the steaming kettle.

"Daddy, what did you call this?" I asked as I mopped up the last
bit of sauce with my bread. "It sounded something like *glumpky*."

"It's a Polish word," he explained. "It's pronounced *go-lomp-ki*,
but it has a funny spelling, g-o-l-a-b-k-i, I think. No *m* in the
spelling." He paused. "I learned a lot of words in different languages
at the store from a lot of nice people." Another pause. "I'm going to
miss that."

When Dad paused for the third time, Bob seized the opportunity
to change the subject. "Do you think teachers should have big tests
on the last day before vacation?" he complained. "No one else is, but
old Bessie Long had to go and spoil it for us."

"*Miss* Long," corrected Dad.

"Wouldn't you rather have it tomorrow than the day you go back
after Christmas?" asked Jeanne.

"He hasn't studied for it, so he doesn't want it at all," said John,
and Bob kicked him under the table. Everybody laughed and Mother
frowned at Bob.

"What did you do all day in Somerset, Daddy?" I couldn't wait
any longer to find out. Somehow, even though he was really touched
by the Zbrozeks' visit, he wasn't sad. He seemed to be in such a good
mood, I didn't understand it at all. He had had an awful week, los-
ing the house and the store and having to pack up and move in such
a short time.

"Well," he said after a sip of coffee, "I had a really good day. First,
I went to the courthouse to take care of store business, and then I

opened an account at a bank." He stopped to take a bite of bread, and we had to wait until he finished it. "Then I went to the high school, Jeanne, to register you and sign you up for your classes."

"Did I get everything that I have at Conemaugh?" asked Jeanne. "Latin?"

"Yes."

"Chorus?" she continued.

"Absolutely."

"Girls' chorus or mixed?"

"Actually," he paused, "you have both. I told the principal it was very important to you."

"Oh, good! Thank you, Dad." She smiled at him and he nodded. "Then," he went on, "I went to your school, Gwen. It has a really nice name, Patriot Street School."

"Won't I go to the same school that Ruth does?" Gwen asked. I could tell she was a little worried. We had always walked to school together.

"No, honey, but you can walk most of the way together, so it won't be so bad. They have a really good playground. You'll like it there, I know. It has first, second, and third grades. I met your teacher, too, Miss Coleman. She seems very nice."

"Okay," she answered, but she didn't seem entirely convinced.

Finally he turned to me. "Ruth, you'll be going to Union Street School. It has just fourth, fifth, and sixth grades. I had a good talk with Mr. Rininger, the principal, and when I told him that you really enjoyed singing in a chorus and being in plays, he told me something that you might find interesting." He stopped and took a bite of stew, then a bite of bread. A spoonful of applesauce followed, then a drink of coffee. It was infuriating. I determined to wait him out.

At last, when he was about to take another bite of stew, I had to give up. "Daddy, please!" I know I sounded exasperated, but I wasn't really. I was so glad to have him back to his old, pleasant, teasing self. "*What* would I find interesting?"

Dad laughed to see that he had aroused my curiosity. "Mr. Rininger told me that they were quite excited at the school because in about a month the music teacher is going to start to work on an operetta."

"What's that?" asked Gwen.

I knew the answer. "It's a play that has a lot of singing in it, Denny. Remember last year when Mr. Border took the choir to Johnstown to hear the Vienna Boys' Choir?" She didn't remember. "Well, they did a short operetta as part of their program." I turned to Dad in disbelief. "You mean they're going to put on an operetta? A grade school?" He nodded, his mouth full again. "But did he say I could be in it?"

"He seemed very sure of it because of your being in Dan Border's chorus," he answered. "Of course, it's up to the music teacher." He was about to take another bite but paused. "Oh, I just remembered something else. I think you'll really like the play. It's about children in an orphanage who raise money by putting on a circus."

He was right. I loved stories about orphans battling enormous odds and succeeding, like Little Orphan Annie in the funnies. "What's it called?" I asked.

"You'll like the title, too," Dad replied. "It's *Sunny of Sunnyside*. Isn't that nice?"

I had to admit that I was captivated.[2] But my father was not finished. "And another thing, Ruth, here at Benson Borough School, you sit in the same seat all day, right?"

"Except for recess," Gwen volunteered helpfully.

"Yes, well, at your new school, Ruth, you'll change classes and go to different rooms with different teachers. Just like in high school. Also, you and Gwen will both have classes in art and music several times a week. What do you think of that?"

I hadn't anticipated such changes at all and couldn't even articulate my reaction beyond nodding and smiling at him. I could tell from his expression that he was pleased to share these bits of news.

Still he was not finished. "I think I've saved the best for last," my father announced. I felt a quick intake of breath. What could be better than having art and music, changing classes, and being in an operetta? But my dad was right, as I eventually discovered.

"I had just come from the Union Street school and parked on the street outside the courthouse. I was looking around to see what was close by. Across from the courthouse on one street was the post office, so I went there and took care of starting up our mail delivery. I went into the courthouse and finished up the store business. As I was coming down the steps, I looked over at the bank on the corner. Something made me glance up at the second floor, and there I saw a sign for the Somerset County *Public Library*!" His voice sounded as though he had discovered a cathedral.

"Did you go up?" asked Gwen.

"Yes, I did," Dad replied. "You should see it! There are about four big rooms with shelves of books from floor to ceiling."

"Are there books for kids?" asked Gwen.

"You bet!" he answered. "There's at least one large room full of children's books. And Ruth, listen: it's on your way home from school! You can stop there every day on your way home."

"Do you just read the books there?" I wondered. That could take a long time.

"Oh, no, you get a library card and you borrow the books you want and return them within two weeks." He reached for the book on the counter behind him. "In fact," he smiled with satisfaction, "I got a library card myself and I took out a book, a collection of humorous essays." He turned the book so we could see the title, *Cream of the Jest*. "It looks good."

By now, everyone had left the table except for Daddy, Gwen, and me. While he took the opportunity to finish his applesauce and coffee, Denny and I talked about going to the library.

"How will I know how to get there? It's close to your school but not mine," she worried.

"We can practice walking to the library next week. I'll meet you there. Or you can meet me at my school and we can walk to the library. Or," I ran through all the possibilities I could think of, "I could walk to your school and we could walk back to the library. We'll work it out, okay?"

"Okay," she agreed, satisfied that I would look out for her.

Here's the reason the library was so important to our father. Fourteen years or so before, our family had moved to Hollsopple from Miller Run for Dad to open the store with Mr. Bailey. As the store became successful, he began to buy sets of books: the *Encyclopedia Britannica*; the *World Book*; the *Harvard Classics*, including works of Shakespeare; the *Literary History of the World War*; and great collections of poetry, plus a large dictionary and an atlas.

In addition, we had a lot of popular series of young people's books about the Rover Boys, the Automobile Girls, the Boy Scouts, the Girls Scouts, the Campfire Girls, Tarzan, the Bobbsey Twins, and many others, not very literary but great fun. It wasn't unusual for people in town to drop in to look something up or to borrow a book. I think all of us grew up loving to read and treasuring books. So, being able to visit a library easily and regularly gave us a promise of a rich reading life.

Gwen wandered away and I was left alone with my dad. Somehow, after all these months of worry, there was a difference in him. The trip to Somerset seemed to have started a change. What was it?

I sat there for a minute or so and wanted to tell him something, to let him know that I had changed, too. "Daddy," I began, "I think it's going to be real nice in Somerset, don't you?"

"Yes, I do," he replied firmly. "I'm glad you feel that way because I was afraid that you were going to be very sad at moving from Hollsopple."

That's funny, I thought. That's what I felt about him. Just then Mother came out to the kitchen.

"It's getting late and the dishes aren't done," she said, but I could tell she wasn't mad or anything. I got up from the table and carried some dishes to the sink.

"Mother, I've been thinking about the Christmas tree," I started to say, "and it'll be okay if we don't have one. It *is* a lot of work for just that one day here."

"Well, we'll see," she replied as she began to fill the dishpan. Then she started a whole new subject. "Ruth, I'm going to make popcorn balls on Saturday afternoon. Would you like to make some for Tootie and Betty Benson and the Shaffers?" Of course, I wanted to.

We worked at packing boxes that evening and didn't get to bed before ten. Gwen and I fell asleep right away, with no talking about moving or school or Christmas or anything. But just before we dropped off, Daddy stuck his head in our door and said, "Did I tell you there's a little orchard of twelve apple trees at our new place in Somerset?" Unbelievable, I thought. And wonderful.

When I woke up in the morning, Gwen had already gone downstairs. I lay there for a few minutes in the chilly room, thinking about everything I had to tell my friends and my teacher about Somerset: the school, the operetta coming up, and the library that was on my way home. I jumped out of bed and got dressed in a hurry. I had a new feeling, not exactly being happy but something else that seemed even better, being…hopeful, I think it was.

I sat down on the edge of the bed and started to brush my hair. I was absently pulling strands from my hairbrush when Gwen appeared in the doorway.

"Hurry up," she said. "Mother says breakfast is ready." She looked at the hair I was rolling into a ball. "What are you doing?"

"Remember what Grandma used to do with her hair?" I asked her.

"Oh, sure," she answered and picked up her brush from the dresser. "Here's some of mine." I rolled the strands of long black hair together with mine and went to the window. I raised it and placed the little ball outside on the ledge and closed the window.

"I don't think there are any birds around now," I said and began to leave. "It's way too cold."

"Ruth, look!" Gwen spoke softly. A small brown bird had landed on the roof. It hopped up to the ball of dark hair, cocked its head to look at it, and suddenly picked it up and flew away. We both laughed, we were so amazed. "I want to tell Mother about it," Gwen said excitedly and ran down the stairs.

That's the perfect goodbye, I thought, leaving something of ourselves here, just like Grandma. I stood at the window a moment longer, looking out over the frozen back yard to the far edge of trees that hid the river. I left the room and went downstairs to join the others. I couldn't wait now to finish the last chapter: the final day of school, the children's concert, presents and Christmas dinner, saying goodbye to everyone, and at last, moving to Somerset.

The house in Hollsopple my family lost in 1938, as it looks today (2003) I miss the catalpa trees out front. Photo by Mary Buckley

Lost Days of Childhood

Lost days of childhood—how sweet they seem!
How fair yet faraway, like some faint dream.
If it could ever be, how we should smile to see,
Running to greet us with eyes full of glee,
Children whose very names mem'ries can stir.
Where are you hiding, O kids that we were?

John and Elizabeth, Bobby and Jeanne,
Ruthie and Denny, oh, where have you been?

RMS

Notes

Chapter 2

1. As you can see from the photograph on page 62, Lady was bigger than today's typical Boston bulldog. Amusingly, her original name was Maggie; we had adopted her and a male puppy and named them Maggie and Jiggs after popular comic strip characters of the time. Maggie soon became Lady, however, when we noticed our neighbor, whose first name was Maggie, appearing on her porch looking rather puzzled whenever we'd call outside for our dog. As I mentioned, Lady was very good-natured. She was smart, funny, easily-trained, and loyal. She even tried to be the mother to kittens our cat rejected.

2. The name of our town is sometimes spelled without the double l; strangely, there seems to be no consensus about how to spell Hollsopple. Maps and other official documents spell it both ways. I chose to spell it with two l's here because that seems to be the original version. I've heard the town was named for a Charles Hollsopple and was spelled unquestioningly with the double l until the railroad came through and erected a sign at the depot that read "Holsopple." Confusion ensued, which continues. The name itself seems to have evolved from the German name *Holz* along with the word for apple, *apfel*, perhaps originally referring to an orchard-keeper. Readers from out of the region are probably most familiar with Appalachian Hollsopple and Somerset County in southwestern Pennsylvania as the site of Flight 93's crash on September 11, 2001, near Shanksville, just ten miles from Hollsopple, and the following summer's rescue of the nine trapped coal miners near the town of Somerset, about twenty miles away. Also, along its western edge Somerset County borders Fayette County, site of Frank Lloyd Wright's Fallingwater.

Chapter 8

1. Like Hollsopple, Stoneycreek has alternate spellings: Stonycreek, Stony Creek, and Stoney Creek.

Chapter 9

1. This and other fascinating information is available from the tour guides and exhibits at the Johnstown Flood Museum. The museum's focus is the 1889 flood, though it also houses material related to the 1936 and 1977 floods.

Chapter 11

1. The creation and expansion of the Pennsylvania Turnpike created great excitement—as well as employment—in the area. John often drove with his bride-to-be, Esther Long, on dates to see the lights and the progress of the road-building on the turnpike. In fact, it was alongside the Pennsylvania Turnpike that John proposed to her! Once my family had moved to Somerset and I was a little older, my friends and I would occasionally drive to a spot near the new Howard Johnson's at the Somerset turnpike exit, leave our car, crawl under the fence, and walk around the building from behind. Afraid we'd get into trouble for not having been driving on the Turnpike, we'd pretend we had just exited the tollroad and talk loudly of where we'd come from and where we were headed, giggling as we ate our ice cream sundaes.

Chapter 12

1. This well-known restaurant still exists, expanded many times over the years. It's still family-owned and famous for its extensive smorgasbord, one of the first establishments in Pennsylvania to offer all-you-can-eat dining. After we moved to Somerset and Dad's health further deteriorated, making him unable to work, Mother went to work as a cook at Oakhurst; she was employed there for over thirteen years, until she and Gwen moved to Ohio with me after I got my first teaching job. Jeanne and I both waitressed at the Tea Room during summers while we were in college, and Gwen worked as what we'd now call a nanny for the children of the owners. Our families are close to this day.

2. I *was* in the operetta and it turned put to be as wonderful as I had imagined it would be. The lead role was played by Betty Jean Long, a cousin of John's future wife, Esther. She was beautiful, talented, and a wonderful Sunny.

To order *Dark Brown Is the River* by Ruth Mugridge Snodgrass, please complete this page (or a copy) and send it along with a money order or certified check to the address below.

Ship to:

(please print)

Name _____

Street or P. O. Box_____

_____

City _____ State _____ Zip Code _____

Dark Brown Is the River $12 each...........$ _____
Shipping and Handling:
   $4 first book ....$ _____

   $1 each additional ....$ _____

Subtotal $ _____
Ohio residents, add 7% sales tax
(on book amount AND S & H costs)...$ _____

Total $ _____

U. S. orders only

Mail to:

M. J. Buckley
1910 N. Eastown Road
Elida, Ohio 45807

Also available at amazon.com